George Glover has spent most of a long life in Shropshire. He is the author of *Shropshire Curiosities* and *Shropshire Eccentrics* and co-author, with J.J.H. Edmonds, of three operettas. A retired schoolmaster, he is an Open University graduate and joint editor of the West Shropshire Talking Newspaper for the Blind.

SHROPSHIRE MURDERS

—◆—

George Glover

ARCH

Published by ARCH,
The Hope, Lyonshall,
Kington, Herefordshire HR5 3HT

Photoset in Mergenthaler Bembo
at Five Seasons Press, Madley, Hereford

Printed and bound in Great Britain
by Biddles Limited, Guildford

British Library Cataloguing in Publication Data
(a CIP catalogue record for this book
is available from the British Library)

ISBN 0 947618 07 4

Contents

Acknowledgements

My gratitude is due to the staff of the Local Studies Library at Shrewsbury, who have been unfailingly helpful during my researches. David and Evi corrected the manuscript and Gill and Alan read it.

The material was extracted and edited from *Watton's Cuttings*, the *Shrewsbury Chronicle*, Eddowe's *Salopian Journal*, Gough's *History of Myddle* and *Death of a Rose-Grower—Who killed Hilda Murrell?* by Graham Smith.

Preface

The majority of Shropshire murderers were otherwise ordinary working folk, whose humble lives are not normally described in a form available to us. They did not write books, keep diaries, or even write many letters. But in courts of law and at inquests, murderers and witnesses had their brief moments of glory, and shame, when they told the world, through the newspapers, what drove them to do what they did. As I skimmed through old newspaper accounts of murders and murder trials, I became aware that they were plunging me into the otherwise undocumented social history of the county.

There is certainly a rich variety of them. Some of these histories will attract your sympathy, others—especially where children or the elderly were victims—your horror and disgust. I hope all of them will serve to broaden our picture of the history of the place in which we live.

The Place of Execution

Whenever a judge at the Shropshire County Assizes had cause to pronounce sentence of execution by hanging, the place of execution he referred to until 1868 was the roof of the lodge of the County Gaol in Shrewsbury. The grisly affair was a public spectacle, intended presumably to be a terrible warning to all those who might be contemplating a similar crime.

The execution had to be carried out as soon as possible after sentence was passed, the next day if it were not a Sunday. During the condemned person's last hours he would have the benefit of the prison chaplain's company in the condemned cell, from which could be heard the hammer-blows of the scaffold's builders. The chaplain would urge them to repent and to pray. This exhortation seems often to have worked; reports say that criminals were usually 'launched into eternity' in an appropriate frame of mind.

The scaffold itself was of very simple construction. There were two uprights supporting a cross beam to which a rope was attached. Beneath the cross beam was a platform, and in this a trap-door on which the condemned person stood. His legs were pinioned and the noose placed around his neck with the knot under the left ear. A white cap, swiftly produced by the hangman, was put over his head.

When the hangman gave the signal the prison officers stood away, the bolt was withdrawn and the body fell, the neck dislocated by the sudden jerk when a certain length of rope had been paid out. It was the hangman's task to calculate the length of drop needed for each individual, depending on his weight and the strength of his neck. (The hangman's perks included the fatal rope, which he could often sell for a considerable sum.) The deed done, the body of the criminal was left hanging for an hour, after which a doctor had to certify that he was dead.

A public execution was treated by many as a spectacle not to be missed. People travelled several miles to be present, arriving early in order to get a good view. One farm worker is reported to have asked his master for the day off to enable him to see the hanging at noon and go on to a football match at two.

Any vantage-point with a reasonable view of the scaffold was in demand. Sometimes there were nearly as many women as men among the gathering, and often children, permitted to group near the front so that they could see clearly all that went on. Usually, but not always, the crowd was on the side of the condemned man or woman.

Edward Cooper of Baschurch

Edward Cooper lost his wife after a short married life, short but long enough for the birth of two children, a boy, John, and a girl, Jane. Making things so much more difficult for this hard-working farm labourer, the son met with a serious accident when a door fell on him. Although intelligent, he was obviously disabled, and was going to find it difficult to earn a living.

Mr Cooper farmed his children out, but his wages were insufficient to pay the maintenance. At one stage he thought of re-marrying, and approached a Jane Sadler, who was servant to the farmer living next door to the farm where John Cooper worked and lodged. She turned him down, because her employer told her that Cooper 'did not bear a very good character'. One wonders what his evidence was and what his motive.

The unhappy Mr Cooper received a further blow when the family looking after John returned him. With the boy he visited the people taking care of Jane. He told them that he had applied to get both children into a workhouse, but they would not take them for less than three shillings a week each, and that amount he just could not afford. After another attempt to settle the boy with his keepers John was returned again to an increasingly desperate father. For a few days the lad lived in a hayloft on the farm where Edward Cooper worked.

On the first Sunday following, Edward got permission from his master to take the boy to Hanwood. He had friends there, he said, who would take care of him. Several people saw the man and boy walking on the way to Hanwood, where they spent the night. They left next day at 7 a.m., and again were seen by several folk on the road, until they were about three-quarters of a mile from home, at a place known locally as the World's End. There farm labourers saw them leave the road and enter an ash plantation.

Some time later Edward Cooper emerged without the dark coat he had been wearing earlier, approached the door of a Mrs Abbots, who lived in one of a row of cottages, and asked for the loan of a spade. He returned the spade later, and went home alone to his master's house. He said he had sent his son with his cousin to Manchester, to stay with a grandmother.

In the following weeks Cooper aroused suspicion among his acquaintances by giving out contradictory accounts of what had been done with the boy. But it was not until two months after the Hanwood expedition that a drinking party in a Baschurch pub took the matter a step further. The Cooper mystery was the topic of conversation when Mr Abbots, who happened to be there, said, in jocular mode, 'I wonder what he wanted with the spade he borrowed at my house—I'll be bound he's buried the lad in the coppy.'

This remark was reported to Sergeant Bullock, who paid a visit to Mrs Abbots. She couldn't remember the date on which Cooper had borrowed the spade, but her neighbour Mrs Walton could. The police superintendent in due course made enquiries at Hanwood; the Manchester tale turned out to be a complete myth.

When arrested Cooper claimed that he'd sold the boy to a travelling tinker for half-a-crown. Then the body was found in the coppice, and the game was up. At the trial the unrepentant prisoner claimed that the crime was all Jane Sadler's fault. The judge and jury felt unable to agree.

Cooper was hanged at Shrewsbury on the 15th of December, 1862, for the wilful murder of his eight-year-old son John. The case made a considerable impact on the public at large, partly because it was the first public hanging at Shrewsbury for nine years, but mainly because it was so very sad.

The Axeman of Clun

During the first half of the seventeenth century, religious controversy was rife in many parts of England. Successive sovereigns had sought to imprint differing interpretations of Christian worship upon their subjects—Protestantism, Papism and Puritanism. Ordinary folk were expected to conform to the rules laid down by their local cleric, which was no problem to the compliant, but could be seriously unsettling for the free thinker. To make matters worse, an Act of Uniformity had made attendance at Sunday services obligatory. Householders could be fined one shilling if any of the family or servants failed to attend.

Enoch Evans, a farmer's son from Clun, found it difficult to accept the religious attitude and observances expected of him. With his father Edward and his brother John, he worked on the farm at Shadwell, but he was often depressed and unhappy over matters of religion. He was fond of reading the Bible at home, and was often withdrawn from the busy life around him.

The family took communion regularly at Clun church, where Erasmus Powell was vicar. Enoch at one point came to the conclusion that kneeling to receive the Holy Sacrament was the incorrect posture; in that attitude the legs were not blessed. His objection led people to regard him as 'a dangerous thinker'.

On one occasion he was found during a cold winter period naked in a brook, his face buried in his hat as if in prayer. The married couple who came across him thus persuaded him to put his trousers on and accompany them quietly home. His father took him to Bishops Castle for a routine blood-letting, and Enoch improved.

On another occasion, when kneeling at the communion rail in Clun church and offered the chalice Enoch ordered the priest to 'fill it up!' The shaken celebrant did so, and Enoch grabbed the cup and downed the wine in one go.

His father was advised to have Enoch 'tutored', and he set him up in lodgings with a Mr Gravenor, a scrivener, or scribe. A few days later a tobacco pedlar arrived, to spend the night at the house. Enoch viewed him with alarm and distrust. During the night the scrivener, hearing someone moving about below, found Enoch in a state of terror. He was convinced that the stranger had been brought from Ireland to kill him. To pacify the poor chap, Mr Gravenor turned his wife out of their bed and instructed her to make a calming brew. He took Enoch to bed with him, and they passed a much disturbed night together. Enoch ran off home at first light, and the scrivener wisely let him go.

One day in May, in the year 1633, Enoch went to Knighton. He was interested in a black ox for sale, he said. He sought out a Margaret Jones, from the Spoad, and took her and a relative to an inn, where he plied them with drinks and spoke long and earnestly with Margaret in Welsh, a language of which the third member of the group had no command. She obviously did not much care for what he had to say, became increasingly restless, and left without ceremony. On the same evening Enoch suddenly took off for Clun. His worried brother John went after him. It turned out that Enoch had wanted Margaret to marry him there. She had agreed, in order to get rid of him, but she failed to appear.

On the following day his father returned home from market at Bishops Castle to find his wife Joan and his son John had been decapitated with an axe. Their bodies lay in a pool of congealed blood, and Enoch was missing. Two sergeants-at-mace found him later the same day at the house of a relative at Guilden Down, one mile north of Clun. They marched him the fifteen or so miles to Shrewsbury, spending a night on the way at the Round House, Pulverbatch, and lodged him in the county gaol.

He was sentenced to be hanged in chains 'in some convenient and eminent spot adjacent to where the murder was committed'. Many local people sympathized with the hapless prisoner, whom they regarded as honest but misguided. After the execution relatives were urged to remove the body from the gibbet, where by law it was supposed to hang until it disintegrated, in order to discourage other would-be felons. His father, who was law-abiding, refused to countenance any such act, but Enoch's two sisters paid a friend of his to take the body down one dark night . They carried it three miles on horseback, then buried it in a sawpit, of which the exact location has never been disclosed.

Brutal Bungler at Eyton

In the second half of the seventeenth century the Earl of Bridge-water owned a large tract of land in the area between Ellesmere and Wem. One of his farms was rented by the Elks family, the last of whom, Hugh Elks, came to a bad end.

He heard that one of his neighbours, who lived in the hamlet of Eyton, kept a large amount of money in the house. With certain companions he conceived a plan to carry out a robbery on a Sunday morning, at a time when all God-fearing people would be in church.

The miscreants wore masks when they entered the house, where they found a servant maid making cheese. As Elks was bending down in order to tie her up she glanced under his mask and recognized him.

'Good uncle Elks, do me no harm', she said. His reaction was to take out a knife and cut her throat.

His terrified accomplices took to their heels, entering the church at Baschurch. Finding himself deserted Elks, too, fled, and left the money where it was. In his panic he closed the door hurriedly behind him, and failed to realize that he had shut his dog in the house. He made his way to his home at Marton, but couldn't settle down there, so he ran to Petton church. Hot and bothered, he slipped inside just before the end of morning service.

The family at Eyton arrived home from church to find the servant girl dead and Elks's dog gorged with the cheese it had eaten. The animal, when released, led them to its master's house. Elks was apprehended on suspicion.

When the coroner opened the inquest on the following day Elks denied any knowledge of the crime. He had been in Petton church, he said, attending morning service. But a servant girl employed by John Ralphs, of Marton, testified that she had heard the entrance gate to the open field bang. Looking through the window of her master's house, she had seen Elks coming from the gate at a time when the service would have been half over.

Elks responded that it was not possible to see the gate in question from any window in that house. The jury then went in a body from Eyton to Marton, and the maid showed them the gate as seen through the window.

The jury subsequently found the prisoner guilty of murder. At his trial he was found guilty, and was hanged at Shrewsbury.

The Longden Murder

Nothing arouses the anger and revulsion of ordinary folk more than the murder of a child. So enraged were the good people of Longden village that twice they were on the verge of lynching John Mapp who, just before Christmas in 1867, brutally murdered nine-year-old Catherine Lewis.

It is difficult in these days to believe how the conditions which made this crime possible could have arisen. Longden, six or seven miles from Shrewsbury, was and is a working village in an agricultural area, the sort of place where all the residents are known to all the others. So everybody must have been aware that John Mapp, a farm labourer, who was still in his early thirties, had served a sentence of transportation for a criminal assault on a married woman. Yet nobody saw any danger in his accompanying this young girl along a quiet lane on a dark winter's night.

It was a Sunday, and Catherine had spent the afternoon with the Davies family, where she had sometimes acted as a servant. In the evening she went to the service at the chapel, a little way outside the village. Mrs Davies recalled pinning her brooch on her shawl before she set out. She was wearing a straw hat, black with a pink ribbon.

After the service Catherine started for her own home in the company of a small group going the same way, a domestic servant and two or three other children. These latter said 'Good-night' at their various homes and lane-endings, until only Mapp and Catherine were left. Shortly after this the man must have attacked the girl for a reason or reasons which didn't emerge in the investigations that followed.

Catherine had often spent the night at the Davies's, so her family was not at all surprised when she did not come home. But the next morning her blood-stained, crumpled hat was found by a very young waggoner stuffed into a holly bush, and two village ladies took it rather fearfully to her home. Her father then went to look for her.

First he came across John Mapp, who was spreading manure near the lane. Had he seen her? No, replied the man. Mr Lewis then crossed two fields, continuing his search, and entered a cowshed belonging to a Mrs Jones, of Shrewsbury, and there he found the dead body of his daughter, in a hayloft. Devastated, he ran out, shrieking with horror, to find help. He met two villagers who came back with him to witness the dreadful scene. Then he went to fetch a policeman. Soon John Mapp was under arrest.

It turned out that he had struck the child a heavy blow about the head, cut her throat, and stuffed part of her shawl into her mouth. Then, probably early on the following morning, he had dragged her by the heels nearly a quarter of a mile to the building where he left her. Why did he attack her? There was no sign of sexual molestation. Had she been impudent? Referred to his past, perhaps? Surely it could not have been on account of the brooch, pretty but inexpensive, which was later found in the murderer's pocket.

At his examination Mapp denied any knowledge of the crime. The girl had walked on, he said, when he turned aside from the lane. He owned a knife, but he had left it at home when he went to chapel. The blood on his clothes had come from a nosebleed, unlikely as it might appear. The brooch? He had bought it, he claimed, from a fellow he did not know and would not be able to identify, on his way home. This in spite of his father's evidence that he was in bed shortly after the crime must have been committed.

The entirely circumstantial evidence was enough to seal Mapp's fate, despite a brave and lucid defence by an advocate nominated by the judge. The jury needed only six minutes to consider their verdict and the judge was so moved by the pity of the case that he had the greatest difficulty in finishing his pronouncement of the awful sentence of death by hanging.

The Witch of Wenlock

In March, 1841, William Davies, a labourer, was living with a very much older woman commonly known as Nancy Morgan, although she had in her time been called other names. Their cottage was at Westwood, just outside Much Wenlock. The unusual thing about this set-up for those days was that the pair were not married, which was not the fault of the lady, often referred to locally as 'the old woman'. Rumour had it that she had had the banns declared in Madeley church, but the matter had got no further than that.

Nancy owned some land, which William dug and planted for her, and it appears that he was looking forward to getting his hands on her money when she died. But when she soon did, William's part in her demise led in very short order to his own.

Nancy had a reputation as a witch, or, at least, a person possessing the evil eye and able to tell fortunes. Many local people were afraid of her on that account and tended to give her a wide berth. William, on the other hand, was regarded as an inoffensive fellow very much under the thumb of his co-habitee and quite unable to shake off her power over him. If he left her, she said, she would draw him back with the use of her supernatural skills. William, rather weakly, believed her.

The pair quarrelled a good deal. At William's trial several neighbours were to testify to bitter disputes, mutual abuse, and the most appalling language. It all came to a head when William had been sent to Much Wenlock to buy some meat. He had spent some of the money she gave him in Wenlock's two pubs, the Bulls Head and the Horse and Jockey, each kept, as it happened, by a different Mrs Aston. The row that developed on his return led to his declared intention, not for the first time, to leave her. Just let him collect his working togs and the watch she had given him. She said the watch was hers, and when her mutilated body was found upstairs it was clasped in the dead woman's hand, her thumb through the outer case and the chain wrapped around her bloodstained fingers. The timepiece cost the purchaser £5 from Mr Glaze of Bridgnorth; it also cost, in the end, two lives.

Dr Brookes, of Olympic fame, was the surgeon called to the scene. He found many head wounds, inflicted with a knife, and the carotid artery was severed. There was blood everywhere. An open knife was found on the kitchen dresser.

Meanwhile, the police set out to chase the missing William, who had locked the door before taking to the open road. Recruiting voluntary helpers on the way, the constables eventually apprehended the fugitive in a barn at the Leasows and took him to the Pound at Leebotwood, whence he was taken back to Wenlock in a spring cart. On the way the suspect, somewhat confused and weary, perhaps—these were the small hours and he'd been through a lot—said of the final quarrel: 'I asked her to kiss me several times', and 'I did love that old woman.'

The prisoner's advocate at the trial made an impassioned speech. The evidence pointed merely to manslaughter, not murder, he said. But the judge would have none of it. It took the jury 25 minutes to find William Davies guilty of wilful murder. He listened to the time-honoured death sentence with stolid indifference, the same attitude he had maintained throughout his trial. Then he walked nimbly down the steps to his cell.

A Life Not Worth a Light at Bridgnorth

'I have lost my life for three shillings.'

In these words John Newton, 40, a farmer at Severn Hall, Bridgnorth, summed up his folly in murdering his wife, Sarah Newton, in January, 1823. To make matters worse, she was pregnant with what would have been their fifth child. In that condition he had struck, beaten and kicked her so viciously that her worst injuries could not be described in court.

On the day of the murder the local tinsmith and brazier, George Edwards, called at the 170-acre farm with his bill. Among the items listed was a lantern costing three shillings. Newton questioned it. He had, he claimed, given his wife the money to pay for it. When he taxed her about it, she left the room and did not reply.

Newton became incensed. She would ruin him, he stormed. She had run him into debt at different times and in different places. He would beat her, thrash her, the big farmer threatened.

Mr Edwards shared a jug of beer with Mr Newton, and stayed for several hours. The farmer's anger at his wife's misdemeanour, as he saw it, did not abate. Edwards remonstrated with him. He ridiculed the idea of beating her for such a trifle. He was prepared to overlook the cost of the lantern, and cross the item off the bill, if that would make him relent.

When Newton told Edwards that his wife was in the family way the tinsmith grew even more apprehensive. He made the farmer give his word that he would not harm her. When he saw her in the kitchen, nursing a child, she looked miserable but not unwell.

In the small hours the farmer appeared at the tinsmith's door. He was looking for Dr Hall's house.

'A bad job has happened,' he said.

Mr Edwards instantly feared the worst. Not that, said Newton. Not from striking—it is the way she was, implying that a problem had arisen connected with her pregnancy.

Mary Jones, a farm servant, had been sent on an errand across the Severn at about four o'clock. She returned at about eight by ferry, and when still four fields away from the farmhouse she heard children cry: 'Oh, daddy, dunna!' Running to the house, Mary found Sarah Newton lying on the ground 'bleeding dreadfully'.

A hue and cry was raised, and within an hour or so servants, workmen and neighbours had assembled around the stricken woman. The regular midwife had been fetched. She told Newton to send for the doctor. He refused.

When William Bache, a farm servant, was sent on that errand he found Dr Hall out, and his assistant Mr Barber came. He ordered the application of vinegar and water to the 'principal seat of the injury'. Only when his wife was pronounced dead did Newton decide it was time to fetch a 'proper doctor'.

Later the farmer confided to Bache: 'I gave her two or three blows, but I gave her no violent blow to kill her.' At the same time he was asking Mary Jones not to say what she knew—not talk about the cries of the children she had heard and whatever his dying wife might have told her.

At the trial the medical assistant Barber cut a sorry figure. When the judge suggested that he should have ascertained the source of the bleeding and tried to stop it his reply was that it was already too late. Her pulse was 30 and she was 'fast sinking into her grave'.

The surgeon who carried out the post-mortem couldn't bring himself to describe the injury which caused death, but there had been several violent blows on various parts of the body.

A plea of insanity was rejected, although seven of Newton's former workers testified that they had formed grave doubts about him. The prisoner's oddities and eccentricities mentioned by them, observed the judge, were commonplace among otherwise normal people.

In gaol the condemned man admitted having often beaten his wife. After attacking her on this last fatal occasion he had in his temper turned on the child who was making a fuss, and the boy only escaped his father's wrath by outrunning him.

A Burgling Blacksmith at Market Drayton

Francis Bruce, farmer, lived with Ann Taylor, an unmarried servant, in the village of Longford, less than a mile west of Market Drayton. In the year 1812 he was doing so well that he had amassed quite a little nest-egg of gold and silver coins. When his friend James Leigh visited him on Easter Day he was told about this hoard, in guineas, half-guineas and seven-shilling pieces, and was shown a handful of the gold, which was kept in a pitcher with a broken brim.

Rowland Preston was a blacksmith, born in Market Drayton. Until the beginning of October 1812 he had been living in London. Unlike Francis Bruce, he was not prospering, so he decided to seek work again in Shropshire, where there were bells to be hung, and in Scotland, on the Duke of Buccleuch's estate, to fit grates. For the journey he borrowed thirty shillings from his landlord's wife. He said he would be back in three weeks.

He surfaced again at Knighton, Ternhill and Drayton, each time in public-houses. In Knighton he borrowed a hammer and chisel from a local blacksmith. He didn't return the tools. Also at Knighton he was afterwards reported seen with two companions, drinking. Each of the men carried a stick. Because the landlord had been asked by the squire to take special note of any customers likely to disturb his game, he looked attentively at this trio, and particularly at the sticks they carried.

On the morning of Sunday, October the 18th, farmer Bruce had a visitor. They dined together on roast mutton and plum pudding. The guest left at three. A couple of neighbours saw and spoke to Mr Bruce and Miss Taylor that morning.

The day after, the house was quiet. On the Tuesday Elisabeth Johnson, a neighbour, tried the door. She could not get in because the peg which lifted the latch was missing. In the cowhouse the three cows were making a lot of noise. The pigs appeared to be hungry. Elisabeth and two other local women milked a cow each and obtained three times as much as at a normal milking.

Then a curious villager called Bradshaw climbed through a hole in the roof of the cowhouse, got into the house on the first floor, and went downstairs to find Francis Bruce and Ann Taylor dead on the kitchen floor. They had each been struck a heavy blow on the skull. Their throats had been cut, the windpipe and arteries severed.

Two men broke down the door. The victims lay as described by the shocked, incoherent Bradshaw. The place had been ransacked and valuables stolen. A stick and a clasp-knife had been left in the kitchen near the bodies, and a second stick was propped up against the wall near the door.

Reports began to circulate in the next few days concerning Rowland Preston's movements. He had been seen running towards Eccleshall on the day after the murder and he had hired a one-eyed man to help him carry a goose in a basket, for his mother-in-law, he had said. He had taken a coach to Birmingham, where he had badly wanted to ride inside, but there was no room. The same thing happened on the London coach which he took in Birmingham. But the most significant information was that he had had money about him. He had paid off two or three debts, he had wanted to change money, and he had foolishly boasted of his wealth.

Preston reached his London lodgings on the Wednesday after the murder. He was arrested on the Saturday and stood trial at Shropshire Assizes on the 20th of March, 1813. His two accomplices do not appear to have been charged.

The witnesses helped to build a formidable case against the accused. He admitted receiving £17 of the loot, which he reckoned totalled £80. But he denied having committed murder. He allowed that he deserved the severest sentence for theft. This being an age when crimes against property were regarded just as seriously as offences against the person, Preston was condemned to death and was hanged in front of the county gaol in Shrewsbury.

Some 20 years afterwards, a dying man at Ellesmere was so tortured by his conscience that he confessed to a clergyman that he was one of the murderers. While Preston stood by the door keeping watch, he said, he and the third member of the party carried out the butchery. But the real killers were never prosecuted.

The Beckbury Butcher

George Hayward, a twenty-year-old butcher, was living in the village of Beckbury in the summer of 1833. He was very interested in one of the Causer girls, who lived with their mother. The daughter he fancied, however, did not like him. So when he called at the house one night in July, he was not welcome.

He had been working on the harvest, and had drunk more than was strictly necessary to wash the dust out of his throat. Mrs Causer, a widow, was not pleased to see him. She sent for her son John, who arrived in about an hour and literally kicked Hayward out of the house. The ejected suitor became threatening. He would make Hayward remember how he had treated him, he said.

John Causer said that he went so far as to take Hayward's hat out to him. Which makes it hard to understand why the discomfited swain should insist on returning to the house later to collect his property.

Hayward lodged with a Maria Meeson. In court she described how she had gone to bed that night fairly early. She heard her lodger come home and enter her house through the window of his ground-floor bedroom, apparently his normal method of ingress and egress. She then heard him go into the pantry. He did not stay there long but left the house again, once more by the window. She went to look out of her window and saw him leave by the wicket. On the street, she heard an argument with Causer about a hat. Then she heard the sound of a blow, and the following exchange:

'Oh, George, what have you done?'

'Jack, I've done the thing that is right.'

The thing that apparently seemed right for George at that moment was to plunge a long, sharp knife—'like a cutlass,' the victim later said—into Causer's belly. It was a bad wound, said Mr Fletcher, the surgeon who came from Shifnal, so bad that the intestines protruded. Not surprisingly, the poor lad complained a lot. He lingered for a few days, then expired.

Hayward's landlady explained in her testimony that her lodger kept his knife, one of three he possessed, in her pantry. He used it to cut up his food. It seemed likely that on the night of the murder his fuddled mind, set on revenge, had led him to collect it for dealing with Causer.

In his summing-up the judge explained that if the jury thought that the offence was committed 'in the heat of blood, before his anger was assuaged,' then it was the mitigated crime of manslaughter. But if the act was coolly and deliberately committed, and intended destruction of the deceased, then it was murder.

The jury returned a verdict of murder. After being sentenced to death. Hayward was apparently unconscious of his 'awful fate'. He was hanged over the lodge in front of the County Gaol.

When Thieves Fell Out at Market Drayton

In the year 1827 there was a great deal of crime in the Market Drayton area. Most of it was theft, in particular sheep-stealing, and a lot of it was the work of one gang whose members were related to each other. John Cox, shoemaker, was the oldest, at 60. Two sons of his, John junior (16) and Robert (19), were associated with him, as were Joseph Pugh (19), Thomas Ellson (23), James Harrison (21) and Ann Harris (60).

When the depredations of this family group had become a serious threat to the community an appeal was made for information. Harrison informed on Ellson, who was arrested, and John Cox junior, who suddenly vanished into thin air. Just before the trial, Harrison went missing. It was assumed that he had been bought off. Since he was the principal witness, Ellson had to be acquitted.

The general assumption was that Harrison had decided to lie low for a while—until Ellson, in trouble for yet another felony, sent for the clerk to the magistrates and offered, in exchange for his release, to reveal all he knew about Harrison's death. The clerk said he would let him off if he would reveal the whereabouts of the body. Ann Harris and Joseph Pugh were arrested.

Ellson's evidence turned out to be flawed, in that the body was not where he said it was. Ann Harris was released, but Pugh was detained. Pugh then in his turn sent for the clerk and made a confession. Taken to a certain field, he indicated where the body lay, fully clothed and much decomposed. It was carefully dug up and taken to the Poorhouse. The surgeon found the body in such a poor state that he was unable to ascertain the cause of death. It was not in a fit condition to wash.

The three Coxes and Ann Harris were apprehended. Robert sought to evade arrest by fleeing to 'a field of standing corn where he stood for concealment'.

But loyalty was not the strong suit of the gang members; a full picture of the events of the night of the murder rapidly emerged.

The victim had been lodging at the house of John Pugh, Joseph's father, but neither he nor Joseph had had a bed to sleep on. When the Pugh parents retired, the two young men were left sitting by the fire in the living room.

About midnight a piercing whistle was heard outside the house. Father Pugh instructed his wife, eight-and-a-half months pregnant, to rise at once and investigate. She went to the window and, there being a full moon, she saw John Cox junior sneaking along in the shadow of the hedge. Soon afterwards, feet were heard moving about beneath.

According to the perpetrators themselves the three young men walked for over a mile away from the cottage to a spot in Maer Lane. There Joseph Pugh suddenly threw Harrison to the ground and John Cox held him down. One of them put a loop of string around his neck and twisted it with a hooked stick until Harrison was dead. Robert Cox, present but a little detached from this brutal act, was said to have carried the shovel for digging the grave. Later, Ann Harris was alleged to have left the shovel outside her back door for the purpose.

The body was buried in a mowing field, but the next morning it was moved to an adjacent ploughed field. At five the next morning, the Pugh parents came downstairs and found their son alone. He told them he did not know where Harrison had gone.

The trial was remarkable in that nearly all the witnesses were related. They seemed to find no difficulty in testifying against each other. Ellson, for instance, was far from reticent about the way in which his own mother, Ann Harris, had plotted Harrison's death, though he must have known that proof of her complicity would ensure her an early visit to the scaffold.

Another witness was able to reveal how the Coxes had discussed plans for getting rid of the informer Harrison. They had considered throwing him into a coal pit, pushing him into a flash while fishing, hiring an assassin to cut his throat, and poisoning him. In the end Ann Harris promised young John Cox fifty shillings to carry out the dirty deed, and she furnished Pugh by way of bribes with meat, shoes, and a smart velveteen coat.

Old John Cox and Ann Harris were charged, not with murder, but with being accessories before the fact. The penalty for that was death by hanging, but the execution would not be immediate; a few days more would be allowed for the condemned to make their peace with God.

All five accused were found guilty and awarded the death sentence, but the old man and his son Robert were reprieved at the last moment. Ann Harris found religion in the condemned cell. She was the first woman to be hanged for twenty-five years. Five thousand people were estimated to have witnessed the execution.

Horrible Murder Attempt at Eyton

As Martha Mason, Dairymaid to Mr Scott, of Eyton, in the Parish of Wroxeter, in the County of Salop, was packing up Butter in a Basket, ready for Market, on the Evening of Thursday, the 30th. of October, 1823, a vile Assassin attempted to murder her, by firing a Gun or Pistol, loaded with Pieces of cut Lead, through the Dairy Window.

The Slugs were principally lodged in the Left Side of her Face and Head, which have deprived her of the sight of her Eye, splintered the Cheek Bone, and caused her Life to be in imminent Danger for many Days. Thus, by the vile Act of some diabolical Wretch, has this honest and faithful Servant been disabled from earning a Livelihood, and that Face, which was reckoned handsome, is now painful to behold; her Mouth, too, can with Difficulty be opened wide enough to receive the smallest Pieces of Food.

The Magistrates of the District, and the Inhabitants of Wroxeter, have hitherto been unsuccessful in their Endeavours to discover the Monster who committed the foul Deed, his Conscience being, at present, his only Accuser.

It is hoped, that a benevolent and charitable Public will pardon the Liberty which is taken in soliciting their Contributions for this unfortunate Female, only twenty-three Years of Age, and by their Aid enable her to procure a few of the Comforts of Life. The smallest Donation will be thankfully received by the Minister and Churchwardens of Wroxeter, and at the Bank of Messrs. Beck, Dodson and Co., Shrewsbury.

(Copied from an original handbill)

A Father's Heinous Crime at Bridgnorth

In 1822 Richard Overfield was thirty-five, working in a carpet factory in Bridgnorth. He was married, with a three-month-old daughter. At about noon one Sunday in September, Louisa Davies, a neighbour, heard what she termed 'heavy screaming' from next door. She ran to investigate. Mrs Overfield was holding the child, both mother and baby apparently in great distress. Three or four other people, including Richard, were already there.

Louisa took the baby and put its mouth to hers. It made her lips smart. She put her tongue into the baby's mouth. It was hot, and tasted sour.

'What have you done to the child?' she asked Richard. 'Nothing,' he replied. 'The cat was on her and I knocked it off.' The baby was taken to a doctor.

The doctor's assistant saw that the baby's mouth was blistered, confirmed the pungent, acid taste with his tongue. He decided that it had swallowed oil of vitriol (sulphuric acid). He called Dr Hall for a second opinion. The two medical men prescribed magnesia in solution, alternating with gruel and water.

Back at home the room was now filled with neighbours. Richard was asked if he had given the child food, or medicine by mistake. No, replied the father, it was the cat. The cat was found and a finger put into its mouth. There was no acid taste there. The house was thoroughly searched. No acid was found. The baby's condition deteriorated and she died at about three o'clock.

On the next day Louisa called on her neighbour again. While she was there the bereaved mother fainted, and the kindly Louisa walked her around the garden to get some fresh air. At the bottom she caught sight of a phial lying on the other side of the fence, retrieved it, and found it to contain a teaspoonful of a dark-coloured liquid. Later, another neighbour remembered seeing Richard stoop at the spot where the phial was found.

He had gone to work as usual on the day after the tragedy. He was well-known, hard-working, and earned eleven shillings a week.

Constable Goodall had the doctors test the liquid in the recovered phial. It was acid sure enough, and Overfield was carted off to Shrewsbury Gaol. His last words to his wife were:

'. . . my dear wench, you have got my watch, keep it for my sake, for I shall never come back, and give my clothes to my poor old father.'

At the trial Mr Southwell, superintendent of the factory where Overfield worked, stated that several gallons of oil of vitriol, used in the plant, were kept in a glass bottle in a small room there. The door was generally kept locked, but there was a communicating door to the yard where Overfield worked. He had discussed the tragedy with the accused, who still maintained that the cat had been responsible, lying on the child's face and 'sucking its breath'. Did he not know the child would be opened? 'Let them do it and they will see,' the man had said.

Dr Hall carried out a post-mortem on the child's body. The results confirmed beyond all doubt that she had swallowed oil of vitriol. A Shrewsbury doctor at the trial had heard, he recalled, of a cat interfering with a baby's breathing and causing death. But the body would in that case look quite different.

After sentence of death had been passed, the judge revealed his knowledge of depositions made before the coroner and deliberately concealed from the jury. Now that they had given their verdict he could say that the unhappy woman was with child by her husband before their marriage. As a result, the prisoner often expressed hatred for her and the infant, saying that he would not 'support the bastard'.

Seemingly indifferent during his trial, Richard Overfield was, while awaiting execution, 'the very emblem of guilt and wretchedness'.

Attempted Murder at Ludlow

The bloody affair at the Angel Hotel, Ludlow, in August, 1840, was one of the most celebrated crimes of the century in Shropshire. The would-be murderer was Josiah Mister, aged 25, an incompetent scrounger from Birmingham. His victim William Mackereth, a commercial traveller from Bristol and a complete stranger. It was Mackareth's misfortune to be in the wrong room at the wrong time.

The man Mister actually wished to murder was John Ludlow, a prosperous cattle-dealer. It is probable that Mister first learned about his quarry from a mutual acquaintance, a Mr Spiers, a Birmingham publican, who would have told him that the cattle-dealer travelled around fairs with ready cash about him.

Mister was hard up and unemployed. He arranged to stay at the Unicorn, in Shrewsbury, where Ludlow was also a guest. Here he ingratiated himself into the company of the commercial room, accepted meals and drinks from others, and left without paying his bill. The evidence at his trial suggested that he had planned to rob Mr Ludlow in Shrewsbury, but his intended victim switched from his usual room to share a double-bedded one with a friend. Mister was able to find out that Ludlow intended to be at Ludlow fair and to stay at the Angel.

Mister walked to Ludlow in time for the opening of the fair. A number of witnesses saw him on the road, where he slept in hay-lofts and cadged meals.

At Ludlow he ascertained that John Ludlow was expected on the Red Rover coach. He awaited its arrival on the other side of the street, then followed closely behind his man to give the impression that they were together. At the Angel he gave out that he and Ludlow were acquainted. As at Shrewsbury, he tagged on to the commercial guests and kept his ears open.

William Mackereth, had also just arrived at the hotel. For some reason Ludlow, who normally slept in room 20, slept elsewhere. Mister was allotted room 17. He retired early. Half an hour later Mackareth was ready for bed. The chambermaid lighted him to his room, number 20, and he locked the door as she left.

At four the next morning Mackereth woke with a start, sensing a hand on his throat. When he tried to brush it away, his fingers found a wet hole. The hands touched him again. He leapt out of bed, sure now there was someone else in the room with him, and tried to open the window to call for help. It did not budge, so he broke a pane and shouted 'Fire!' He then groped his way to the door, along the passage and down the stairs, shouting the alarm. Then his voice grew weaker and he could barely make a sound. First to appear was the one-armed landlord, Mr Cooke. Mackareth was pouring blood from wounds in the face and neck. Cooke instantly assumed that this gory guest had cut his own throat.

Other guests now emerged. They feared that Mackereth could be mortally wounded and decided it would be prudent to take his deposition. They propped him up in bed and, partly in whispers, partly in writing, his story was put together.

Not only had his throat been cut, but another slash across his mouth extended from ear to ear. The surgeon closed the wound with ligatures.

A careful search was now made. There was blood all around the room. A shocked reporter described how the poor man's arteries had jetted blood all over the walls, the window, the door of his room, and the walls and floor of the corridor and stairs. There was a hunt for the murder weapon. At six a.m. a black-handled razor was found by Police Officer Hammonds in the yard outside. Still wet with blood, it seemed to have been flung from Mister's window, where the curtains carried bloody fingerprints. Mister aroused strong suspicion by not joining in the searches. He was in bed, apparently asleep.

Under the wounded man's bed were marks suggesting that some person had been lying there for some time. Since the door had been locked the night before and open in the morning, the assailant must have stowed himself there before Mackereth retired.

Further investigation revealed that Mister had a bloodstained shirt and handkerchief, still moist where laundering had been attempted, and his white cotton stockings were missing. He had alum in his possession, used to take the colour out of bloodstains, and he had been seen going downstairs with a bundle concealed under his clothing. There were splashes of blood leading directly from the victim's room to the door of the suspect. A policeman sent to search Mister's Birmingham lodgings found one of a set of black-handled razors missing.

At the trial, Mister was sentenced to death.

Several people, the condemned man included, drew up petitions for the sentence to be commuted to something less severe because of Mister's extreme youth and the fact that his victim did not die as a result of the attack.

The customary vast crowd attended the execution. Many farmers were asked by their servants to let them have a holiday on that day to see the hanging at noon and go on to the circus at two.

Mackereth survived, though scarred for life.

Shot in the Dark at Nesscliff

At the beginning of 1854 John Gittins, labourer, occupied a cottage in Nesscliff alongside the Holyhead road. With him lived two lodgers, one being John Lloyd, blacksmith.

The two men got on well together until Mrs Gittins gave birth to her last baby. The infant made a lot of noise in the early morning and Gittins suggested to Lloyd that he should rise and see to it, as it was his child. Lloyd strongly denied that any improper intimacy had taken place, and threatened to give Gittins 'a good lacing'.

The resentful Lloyd collected his scythe, squared his account, and left the next day. But he was certainly not prepared to leave it at that.

Either he was deeply hurt by a false accusation or he was most unhappy about his separation from Mrs Gittins. Whatever the case, during the next few days he planned revenge. He collected equipment for the gun he had previously borrowed—shot, caps, and cleaning materials—almost as if he were deliberately scattering clues around the village.

At five a.m. on the last day of February Gittins came downstairs, with his son, to dress for work. As he was leaning forward to lace up his boots, someone fired a gun through the kitchen window at the rear of the house. Gittins received most of the charge in his head.

Remarkably, he refused to accept that he was hurt for some hours. He died in the Salop Infirmary ten days later.

Despite the best efforts of defending counsel Lloyd was found guilty. There was much circumstantial evidence, and the prisoner had made several unwise remarks to villagers at various times.

At his execution, the new railway station in Shrewsbury meant that the usual viewing area was restricted, and the Dana steps were barricaded for fear that the weight of the gawping crowd should cause it to collapse.

Murder and Rape Attempt at Stokesay

Just before midnight on a February night in 1842 Diana Biggs and her children were asleep in their cottage at Stokesay when there came a knock at the door. The visitor asked for a drink of cider. From her upstairs window Mrs Biggs identified the caller as John Jones, cowman, who had been living at Craven Arms. She had no cider, she said. He then asked for water. He said he was lost and 'ready to drop'.

The kindly woman bade her twelve-year-old girl put on some clothing. She was to let him in and give him a drink of cider washings.

Once admitted, Jones became aggressive.

'Is your father at home?' he wanted to know. The father was away working at Clungunford and came home but once a week. Would it be all right if he sat by the fire until morning? No, replied the girl's mother. She would 'have a noise' with her husband if he did. But James Parry, only a hundred yards up the road, would surely put him up for the night. This did not appeal to Jones.

'I won't go out,' he said. 'I'll come to bed.'

'All the beds are full,' declared the flustered mother.

'Then I'll come to bed with thee.'

He went upstairs with the candle the girl had lit, smoking his pipe, and drew aside the curtains of the tent bedstead where Mrs Biggs and her niece, aged 16, were sitting up, and a four-month-old baby was asleep. There was alarm and dismay among the children in the adjoining bedroom. A nine-year-old boy jumped out of bed, intending to fetch James Parry, but the intruder barred his way.

Jones then went downstairs, only to bolt the door outside and return. Despite Mrs Biggs's protests he got into bed beside her. When she called for help he took out his clasp-knife, opened it, and stabbed her several times in the chest. Then he tried, unsuccessfully, to rape her.

By now the terrified children were screaming with fear. The older girl slipped out of the room, ran downstairs and could be heard unbolting the door.

Harassed by the shrieking of the children and Mrs Biggs's resistance the attacker threatened to murder them all. Meanwhile the mother had seized the blade of his knife with one hand and his frock with the other and was hanging on desperately.

Jones now realized that the girl had left the house. He called her back, then followed her down and out into the road. Mrs Biggs, exhausted with her struggles and bleeding profusely, listened for the girl's screams, which mercifully did not come. Shortly afterwards James Parry arrived and then his wife, who kept her company until morning.

A surgeon came to deal with Mrs Biggs's wounds. Superintendent Lewis pursued the assailant to Ludlow, Hereford, Abergavenny, Newport, and Pontypool, where he had fifteen constables round a mine, where the fugitive was thought to be hiding. Meanwhile, Mrs Biggs was starting to make a good recovery.

Jones was eventually arrested in Dudley. Crowds of Ludlow folk awaited the Birmingham Mail opposite the Borough Gaol when the prisoner was brought back. They were after his blood.

Indicted on charges of stabbing with intent to murder, and rape, Jones admitted only the second. The knife had fallen out of his pocket, he said.

He was found guilty on both charges and transported for fifteen years. Mrs Biggs was granted a gratuity of £5 for her conduct and Superintendent Lewis £3 5s, plus expenses, for his exertions in pursuing the prisoner.

Brutal Murder at Bronygarth

On the very edge of north-western Shropshire at the end of 1841 there lived Emma Evans, a respected middle-aged spinster. She had managed the prosperous little shop in the village of Bronygarth for over thirty years. Although there were other dwellings nearby, she was in the habit of keeping her doors bolted, opening up only when customers knocked.

One December evening two men knocked and called out, requesting tobacco. When Emma let them in, they threw her to the floor and began to search her clothing for money. She resisted and screamed. One of her attackers kicked her on the head to quieten her. Then she was beaten with a heavy poker and while one stood by the door to make sure the coast was clear, the other cut her throat. The two ruffians hurriedly grabbed some valuable odds and ends including some pieces of silver, a shawl and a silk handkerchief, and tied them up in a bundle.

They slunk off with their loot, walked fast along the road towards Llangollen, crossed the aqueduct at Pontcysyllte and stopped at the Kings Head at Cefn Mawr. Here they left their bundle outside in the brewing kitchen while they ordered ale to be warmed and bacon fried—bacon they had stolen from their victim.

The landlord's son, William Bradley, and his mother, cooking the bacon, were uneasy about this pair, who were being pressed by the regulars to sing. They may not have felt much like singing; the more talkative of the two pleaded a cold. During these exchanges William went out and inspected the bundle. It was tied tightly, but certain surprising articles could be identified. When the men left he voiced his doubts about them, and he and his brother-in-law set off in pursuit. Finding themselves pursued, the men dropped their bundle and ran.

Back at Bronygarth genuine customers, one carrying a lantern, had found Emma's door ajar and got no reply to their shouts. Stepping inside, they had found the mangled body of the shop-keeper and raised the alarm.

The local butcher galloped away to fetch the surgeon from Chirk, who notified the nearest magistrate, Viscount Dungannon, of Brynkinalt. News of the outrage spread like wildfire.

Suspicion fell immediately on two well-known characters from Wrexham—John Williams, a Cornishman, and William Slawson, tailor. These gentlemen were away from home; it was generally believed that they were being concealed by friends. Rewards were offered for information and all police offices were alerted.

The suspects turned up after a couple of weeks in Coventry, where Slawson had tried to sell eleven silver spoons marked E.E. to a silversmith. The Shrewsbury police were informed and the two men were brought by rail to Wolverhampton, Greyhound coach to Atcham, and chaise to the county town, where they were accommodated in the gaol awaiting examination.

A niece of Emma's identified all the contents of the bundle as having belonged to her aunt. Slawson claimed that they had found the bundle on a footpath near Llangollen. The spoons had fallen out and Williams had pocketed them. He couldn't remember how they had acquired the silver tea-caddy.

Williams attempted to escape from his prison cell while awaiting trial. He extracted a staple from which his hammock was hung and with it removed some bricks from the wall.

Both men made confessions independently. They were inclined to blame each other for the crime. Williams hoped to earn transportation, but no promises were made.

At the Crown Court Slawson had counsel to defend him, Williams not. The lawyer argued that his man was intent only on robbery, and had not envisaged the possibility of murder. Perhaps as a result of this plea, Williams was found guilty of murder, Slawson only of robbery. Williams was sentenced to death, Slawson to transportation for seven years.

Williams claimed that it was unfair that his partner should escape so lightly. Society in general agreed. Williams had been responsible for the actual killing, but Slawson had planned the robbery and delivered the first blow.

At the execution the English and Welsh bridges were so crowded with spectators that horses and carriages were unable to pass. According to a contemporary newspaper report, 'An

immense number of young girls and mere children planted themselves immediately in front of the gallows, and whiled away the
hours in singing and talking—the songs and conversations being
the reverse of improving.'

Taylor, the Stourbridge razor-grinder, was the hangman.
Afterwards the head of Williams was cast in plaster of Paris
by the Coalport China Manufactory and his body was buried in
prison ground near the Beckbury butcher.

The Plight of the Pontesbury Prostitute

A singularly cold-blooded murder took place in the 'secluded village' of Pontesbury in July, 1845. Elisabeth Preece, who lived there at that time, was a woman of questionable virtue. Unmarried, she had had two children and was enceinte for the third time.

She had approached her regular midwife, who had asked who the father was. Never mind, said Liz. He was a good father, and he was going to allow her two shillings a week, so that she would have no need to trouble the parish for assistance.

On her last night she had an appointment with her paramour. Before she left home, she peeled some potatoes and asked her brother to boil them before she got back. She was off to take a letter to the post at Pontesford. On the way she met an acquaintance of hers with whom she exchanged a few words. Then she vanished.

On Sunday morning, a collier known locally as Jasper noticed that the cabin doors of the coal pit sixty yards from the Nag's Head were open. He went to investigate and found female garments. Aware that Elisabeth had been notified as missing from home, he suspected that she must be in the pit. And there, indeed, she was found, her head a shapeless mass.

At the coroner's inquest the preconceived opinion of the affair was that it was suicide. But the cabin doors had been locked on the Saturday night and the key hidden. The woman's companion had searched for and found the key, and there were marks where the body had been dragged to the mouth of the pit. In the cabin were found Elisabeth's bonnet, her cap, and her pockets, ripped from their strings.

Two boys came forward to say that they had heard screams and protests. Two girls reported seeing a well-dressed stranger seemingly anxious to remain inconspicuous. But no arrest was reported. It is possible that the lady's reputation meant that local indignation and compassion—though not horror—evaporated with unusual speed.

The Knockin Shoe-Maker

Thomas Elkes, a journeyman shoe-maker from Knockin, was his mother's favourite son. Elkes had extravagant tastes, and his mother supplied him with money to enable him to indulge them.

His elder brother married and a son was born to his wife. Then both parents died, and the grandmother was made the boy's guardian.

Eventually the grandmother became poor, and the flow of funds to Thomas dried up. He began to suspect that his brother's child might come between him and his estate, so he decided to make away with him.

He enlisted a poor lad from Knockin village to help him. This child was instructed to entice Thomas's nephew into a cornfield, where the crop stood tall, to gather flowers.

Thomas met the two children in the field and sent the poor boy home. His nephew he carried in his arms to the bottom of the field where he had concealed a pail of water. He held the boy's head under the water until he drowned.

Later that day the child was reported missing and a search was mounted. Then, the boy who had led the victim into the cornfield told his story and on searching the field the body was found. It is not clear if it was buried, or had been hidden in the corn for burial on the following day.

Thomas, realizing that the game was up, fled along the London road. Aware of the direction he had taken, the villagers despatched two men after him on horseback. As they passed through Hertfordshire they saw two ravens perched on a haycock, pulling at the hay with their beaks and making an unearthly noise.

Mystified by this behaviour, the two searchers dismounted and entered the field. Thomas Elkes was there, fast asleep on the hay. He was arrested.

Tormented by a guilty conscience, he confessed that the same two ravens had followed him from the moment he committed the crime. Brought back to Shrewsbury, he was tried, condemned, and hanged on a gibbet on Knockin Heath.

The Wellington Wife-Beater

Ann Gregory's last day had started badly. For her husband William, aged twenty-nine, went early to work as usual from his home at Wellington to the Lawley ironworks, where he was a furnaceman. He was disgruntled because his wife had been late bringing him his breakfast. He 'abused her greatly' and threatened to kill her come night. She replied with some spirit, and flung a sizeable piece of clinker at him before she broke off the quarrel and left.

By the time he came home, William's temper had improved. But before long there was renewed quarrelling and screams of 'Murder!' so shrill that the neighbours came in to see what was going on.

They found Ann sitting on the floor with her back against the wall. She soon became unconscious, and died in a quarter of an hour. William, meanwhile, was sitting by the fire with a child on his knee. When they told him that he had killed his wife he leapt to his feet, became emotional, and ran for a doctor.

The two surgeons who came examined the body and reported that they had found 'extravasated blood' on the brain and in the chest. Either, they said, could have been fatal.

There was no external mark of violence and, although a witness had seen William kick his wife, there was no proof that this had been the cause of death.

The judge directed the jury to acquit him of the charge of murder. But he gave him a severe lecture and six months in gaol, to 'provide time for him to reflect,'he said. Only at that point did the prisoner show remorse for what he had done by breaking down and weeping bitterly.

The Whixall Apple-Dumpling

Thomas and Mary Harries lived in Whixall with Mary's parents and Thomas's two children by his first wife. It was not a happy household, apparently because Thomas resented his mother-in-law's harsh treatment of the children. He had been several times heard to mutter that one day he would pay the old lady out for her interference. So when she suddenly became ill one night in December, 1841, with dreadful stomach pains, and went up to bed and died, local people suspected that her son-in-law had murdered her.

The surgeon who carried out the post-mortem on the body of the deceased found corrosive poison in the stomach. She had eaten a generous helping of apple dumpling. When he and the local chemist, Mr Groom, examined the foodstuffs in the kitchen store they found arsenic mixed with the flour.

The Harries family and Mary's parents used the same kitchen, but dined at separate tables. Their custom was to keep a large bag of flour in the larder and from it to replenish when necessary the two smaller bags, one for each unit, suspended from a beam. A few feet away on the same beam, hung a bag of arsenic, used as rat poison. Somehow a quantity of arsenic had found its way along the beam and into the parents' flour bag.

On the night before the tragedy, the grandfather had eaten a pig's fry. Flour had been used to thicken the gravy served with it; after his meal he had been very ill, but recovered. So when on the following night his wife tucked into the apple dumpling he had eaten none of it, not having regained his appetite.

This sudden death, with its disturbing overtones, generated alarm and considerable gossip in the village. The Bronygarth murder (q.v.) not many miles away from Whixall on the county border had only very recently caused a sensation. The coroner, John Dicken, had only just returned home from the sickening spectacle at Bronygarth when he was summoned out again, to Whixall.

Casual remarks and inconsequential actions in the Harries home became suddenly invested with sinister meanings. On the day after the death someone had offered the unconsumed apple dumpling to the children; this had appeared to arouse extreme alarm in their father. Furthermore, he had been observed tidying the kitchen store in a suspicious manner.

A visitor who did accept the uneaten dumpling took it home and gave it to her son, a worker on a canal boat. It made him desperately sick and he died soon after the vessel had crossed the county border into Cheshire.

At the inquest the jury found no difficulty in concluding that Mary's mother had been poisoned. Both she and her husband were charged with the murder and committed to the next county assizes, where they were both acquitted.

Child Murder at Church Stretton

Mary Rogers, aged 28, was living at Wistanstow in 1852. According to her mistress, Mrs Lucas, she was an excellent servant. When Mrs Lucas observed that Mary was pregnant, she expressed her willingness to keep her in service after her confinement.

For this event Mary went to the Evans family at the Round House. A son Edwin, was born. Mary returned to work.

She visited the child once or twice in the first few weeks of his life. Then, on the 23rd of June, she asked her mistress for leave to go and see the baby. Mrs Lucas preferred her to go the next day. At the Evans house Edwin was sent for and the nurse brought him to his mother, who said she wanted to take him to her brother's at Church Stretton.

Mrs Evans' daughters, Mary and Martha, also had business at Church Stretton, and it was decided that the three ladies should walk there together. They shared the burden of carrying the child. Edwin was a chubby, healthy boy, and he slept peacefully for most of the way. The journey took them one and a half hours.

The Evans sisters had to call on a Mr Lewis when the trio reached Church Stretton. Mary, with her baby, turned off down Lake Lane, leading to Hope Bowdler and the house of her brother.

Not many hours later a baby was found drowned, in a pool along Lake Lane. Investigations disclosed that Mary Rogers had no brother. The next day she was arrested.

At the trial Mary Evans testified that on her return journey, half a mile from home, she was overtaken by Mary Rogers, who no longer had the child, and was non-committal when asked where she had left him. It was assumed that he had been kept by the brother, Mr Rogers of Chelwick.

The accused was described as slender with a swarthy complexion and an innocent face, plain and oval. In court she wore a plain dress, a black and red plaid shawl and a white straw hat with a black ribbon, which was rather dirty. She kept her head lowered, as if ashamed, but nevertheless seemed unaware of her true predicament.

Fracas in Shrewsbury Market Square

One Wednesday night in October, 1856, at about 10.30 p.m., a large number of young people were dancing in the Market Square, Shrewsbury, to the music of an itinerant band. Among them was a popular lady named Ann Usher, known locally by her many friends as Annie Laurie. Until a year previously she had co-habited with a John Hollis, better known as John Williams. Ever since she had left him he had pestered her to resume their former relationship—so ardently that she had become afraid of him.

On this occasion she happened to be dancing with a Frederick Clewitt, when her ex-partner stormed up to the couple and demanded: 'What bloody game do you call this?'

There was an altercation. Some punches were slung, some kicks delivered, not all by the men.

Ann seized an opportunity to break away from the brawl and crossed the square to the front of the Plough Inn, where she met Benjamin Bromley, another acquaintance, and told him what had been happening. Others joined them. It was decided to face up to Williams and support the girl. The quarrel developed into an ugly confrontation between Williams and Bromley, both of whom, as it happened, had only one good arm.

An engine-driver called Hopwood knocked Williams's hat off. As he bent to pick it up he fell, possibly because Ann had clouted him with a heavy door key. Here Williams was seen to withdraw a knife from his clothing, open it with his teeth and slip it, still open, into a readily accessible pocket. He probably had it in his hand again when he struck Bromley in the chest, for that gentleman reeled and fell speechless into the gutter. At the Infirmary it was confirmed that the man was dead and that a deep wound near his heart had been the cause.

The police found Williams in the Yard of the Crow Inn in Frankwell. He had no knife about him then. Had he pitched it into the river as he crossed the bridge?

The inquest at the Salop Infirmary was followed by an examination at the County Hall. There not having been a murder in the county for some time, the public displayed intense interest in the case.

The judge heard plenty of evidence, but said that he was not at all sure of the respectability of some of the witnesses, whose depositions tended to be rambling and inconsistent. There was no doubt that the prisoner struck the fatal blow, but where was the knife? Did he strike in hot blood, fearful that the other men were about to attack him? If so, it was manslaughter.

The jury were out for ten minutes and returned a verdict of manslaughter. The crowd applauded, which annoyed the judge intensely. Before he passed sentence, a Mr Kettle begged leave to speak on the prisoner's behalf, since the man had not had the benefit of counsel to advise and support him. He had good references from two previous employers for whom he had worked for a total of six years as a domestic servant. Then he had contracted scrofula, tuberculosis of the lymphatic glands, which made him unemployable. The enforced idleness had led to his getting into scrapes several times.

He was sentenced to fourteen years transportation.

Dreadful Crime at Dorrington

On Thursday morning last one Mary Davies, who kept a little Shop at Dorrington, was found murdered in her House. The Shop not being opened as usual, the Neighbours went to see what was the Matter, and finding the Back-door open, went in, and found the Unfortunate Woman dead on the Floor, with her Brains knocked out with a Coal-axe, and a large Coal put on her Head.

The Coroner's Inquest brought in their Verdict. Wilful Murder by a Person or Persons unknown. And on Wednesday Night one Sarah Turner (otherwise Marygold), who had been several Times in Gaol, and whipt last Quarter Sessions, was apprehended in Shrewsbury, on a strong suspicion of being the Murderer. She had declared her Intentions to a travelling Man the Saturday before, and asked him to assist her in the Business, as there was a good deal of Money in the House. She was drinking at a public House on the Road 'till after 11 o'Clock on Monday Night, had no Money to pay her Reckoning; but returned the next Morning about Ten o'Clock with plenty of Money, and was traced from Dorrington to Shrewsbury.

She has been examined three Times before the Magistrates at the Exchequer, and was on Friday Night committed to the County Gaol of Shrewsbury, to take her Trial at the next Assizes. She . . . received Sentence of Death, (to be hanged this Day and her Body given to the Surgeons to be dissected) . . . Her Behaviour at the Place of Execution was collected and becoming a Person in her unhappy Situation. She acknowledged the Justice of her Sentence.

Sarah Turner's confession: She went to the house of the deceased at two o'clock in the morning, and called her up, it being a lodging-house. She was admitted and given a bed. At four a.m. she rose and went upstairs to see if there was anything she fancied. Disappointed, she went back to bed.

The 'old woman' was called up at six. At eight she told her lodger to get up. Sarah declined, saying she was tired, but nevertheless she did get up. With a reaping hook she cut a cord which was strung across the room. Finding the deceased sitting alone by the kitchen fire she put the cord twice around her neck and strangled her until she thought she was dead. But she began to recover and earnestly begged her assailant to spare her life. Sarah, afraid now of being caught, dragged her victim to the coalhouse and battered her about the head with the coal-axe.

She then robbed her of £7 7s and twelve half-crowns, and left by the back-door. She made her way to Shrewsbury, where she was apprehended, drunk, on the evening of the following day.

(From Watton's Cuttings, May 1787)

Brutal Highway Robbery at Petton

Mr Woodward, a malt-mill maker, and his nephew Mr Urwick were returning in a gig from Wrexham Fair to Shrewsbury when they were set upon by a gang of determined ruffians near Petton. The attack took place on the 23rd March, 1826, not long after darkness fell. The five robbers carried bludgeons, poles five or six feet long. They lay in wait for the gig and frightened the mare by placing a holly bush in the road. When the gig came to a halt, they belaboured the hapless occupants so fiercely that one of them, at least, could have died as a result. His assailant seemed about to put a knife to his throat when horse's hooves were heard approaching, and the blackguards leapt over the hedge and made off.

The travellers were robbed of all the valuables they had, including £50, a silver watch and a silk handkerchief. The thieves paused in an adjacent field and divided up the spoils. The unconscious victims of the crime were left lying in their own blood. Fortunately, they were quickly found and given succour. Mr Woodward had resisted the initial attack with great courage. He had clung like a limpet to one of the gig lamps and in order to detach him the members of the gang had had to lift up one wheel of the vehicle.

He was taken to the house of Mr Roberts, in Burlton, and then brought home to Shrewsbury by the Bang up Coach. He was very ill for a month after the attack. Mr Urwick, who came out of the ordeal rather more lightly, was most concerned about the loss of a silver watch he had been carrying, that he had borrowed from his uncle's servant, Mrs Priest.

During the hullabaloo that followed the attack it transpired that the miscreants had been seen by local people on thirty occasions since midday. But it was not until a fortnight later before the gang was caught.

A man entered the shop of pawnbroker Fisher, in Deansgate in Manchester, offering a silver watch as a pledge. Fisher's wife was suspicious and sent for her husband, who kept the customer talking. It came out that a second man in the street was offering a silver snuff box. Fisher spotted a watchman passing by and called for help. His suspect was apprehended. Another three gangsters were reported in the Fox public-house. Mr Green, keeper of the Knot Mill Lockup, smartly arrested all of them.

On examination at the New Bailey it turned out that the Petton Five were part of a gang of eight, all Irishmen, who had been roving around the countryside robbing well-heeled travellers. They were said to have the appearance of muscular pig drovers. Their pockets yielded a rich assortment of money, gold and silver watches, silk handkerchieves and knives. One man claimed that he did not know the other four, one said he had found the watch he was carrying, and a third claimed he had not had the tinder box which had just been taken away from him.

The men were being charged with several crimes in different places. But only at the Petton incident could all five be clearly identified, so the wretches were bundled into a coach and brought to Shrewsbury. As their coach approached the town at eight p.m. they were met by several thousand people, who greeted them with threats and abuse.

Charged with brutal assault, amounting to attempted murder, and robbery, the jury found all five guilty. One of them, McGuire (alias Curtis) had confessed to his escort on the journey from Manchester, but Mr Thomas was unable to promise him any leniency as a result. He and two others were sentenced to death by hanging. The other two were transported for life.

On the day of the execution, a Saturday, the local press reported that from daybreak until the fatal hour crowds of people from all parts poured into the town, particularly from the collieries about Wellington, Ironbridge, Shiffnal, and even from Bilston (Staffordshire). A great number of carts, waggons, and other vehicles, chiefly loaded with females, also arrived . . . It is calculated that not less than 10,000 persons were present.

The prisoners rose at four and took the sacrament at 7.30. At about nine the irons were struck off from their legs, and they exchanged prison dress for their own clothes. The final act of the drama took place, as usual, on the roof of the prison lodge.

The two brothers and McGuire died hard, striking their breasts many times after the platform had sunk. The bodies were left to hang, as was customary, for one hour. In the evening plaster casts were taken of the heads by a Manchester phrenologist. The bodies were buried in St Mary's churchyard on the Monday at eight a.m.

No less than three-quarters of the spectators were women. Some were asked: 'Why do you attend executions?'

Their reply was: 'People tell us that if we once see an execution we shall not be hanged ourselves.'

Murder in a Field of Hemp

On Monday last a Murder was committed at Pimley Farm, near Shrewsbury, on the body of one Edward Roberts, a young Man about 19 Years of Age, in the following Manner:

Three Men, viz. John Jones, John Lloyd, and Edward Hughes, of Cysslltu Bridge, near Chirk, in Llangollen Parish, having been reaping at the above Farm all Day, were paid off at Night, after which they endeavoured to pass through a Field of Hemp to get into the Road, which the Occupier of the Farm seeing, sent the Deceased and another Lad, to desire them to come back, and go through the Fold; and they, being obstinate, refused to return, and John Jones took a reaping hook from One of his Companions, struck one of the Lads, and cut him badly over one of his Eyes. The Lad still following them, the said Jones struck Roberts on the top of the Head with the Hook which entered his Brain, of which he instantly died. The Coroner's Inquest gave a Verdict, Wilful Murder, committed by the aforesaid John Jones, who has hitherto escaped the Pursuit that had been made after him.

(From Watton's Cuttings, undated)

Sudden Death in a Bromfield Cellar

At the time of the Ludlow point-to-point race in October, 1784, Mrs Green, the wife of John Green, mason, and Bromfield parish clerk, was found murdered in her cellar. She had been shot. The ball had passed through her head and entered a cask of beer, and it seemed from her position that she must have been shot while drawing beer from the cask.

Her husband had earlier set out from the house to go and watch the race, with a servant boy. During the races he had slipped back home (he had told the boy) to do something he had forgotten.

It appeared that there was a murderer on the loose. At Mr Green's request an advertisement for his capture was put out, offering a reward of £50.

At the coroner's inquest the next day, there was concern about Mr Green's slipping home during the race. It was also considered odd that in the house several boxes had been broken open but nothing stolen. These facts, together with 'other circumstances', led to Mr Green being 'violently suspected'. He was arrested and consigned to Ludlow Gaol.

At a subsequent examination it transpired that a gun belonging to a gentleman lodger at the house had been used since it had been recently cleaned by a gunsmith. The owner declared that it had not been fired to his knowledge. Suspicion mounted. Then Green's brother-in-law produced a letter in which he asked him to testify that he had used the gun to kill a pigeon. As a result, the suspect was transferred to Shrewsbury Gaol.

At the next Shropshire Assizes Mr Green was convicted of wilful murder and sentenced to death. He was hanged at the Old Heath, Shrewsbury.

The Stirchley Murder

One November day in the year 1846 a Mr Clarke, staying at Stirchley Hall, went shooting over the estate. He started a hare in a field, followed it, and came upon a pickaxe lying in the grass. Further on, he was shocked to find a body lying in a deep ditch.

It was the body of a man, on his back as if laid out for burial, partly covered with brushwood and couch-grass. Mr Clarke went away to report this ghastly find. Eventually P.C. Purchase arrived at the scene to make an examination. A business card in one of the pockets was in the name of Zusman, agent or traveller for a Mr Cohen, jeweller, of Birmingham. The man seemed to have been shot as he climbed over a nearby stile. There was much clotted blood near the wound. The corpse had been there for about a fortnight, and had been somewhat gnawed by vermin. The torn leaf of a prayer-book on the grass suggested that the paper had been used as wadding for the fatal gun shot.

The inquest was held at the Rose and Crown Inn. Mr Cohen, Zusman's employer, identified the body, as did Aaron Gottheimer, keeper of the Crown at Ironbridge, where the deceased had lodged. He had been sent to travel around Ironbridge, selling mainly watches and chains. These goods, worth some £420, he carried in trays in a black leather case.

It was part of his duty to write a letter every night on his progress, and report personally to his employer in Birmingham every Friday. There came a week-end when he failed to appear, so Mr Cohen had gone to look for him. Not being able to find him, he had taken a warrant for his arrest.

During the investigations, certain people reported having seen Zusman in company with George Harris, a chain-maker from Dawley, and Richard Hart. Others remembered Harris being in possession of watches and chains, though he had previously been hard up. In fact, he had bought a silver watch from the deceased and paid only 10/- of the £27 12s purchase price. It became apparent that he had told a number of lies. Suspicion darkened about him.

When Hart and Harris were brought to trial Hart was acquitted early in the proceedings for lack of evidence. With Harris, the crucial factor was the time of the murder—noon or evening. He had a cast-iron alibi for the evening, and Zusman was reported as having been seen during the afternoon.

The judge in his summing-up leaned strongly towards the later time, a November dusk with very few people about. A shot had been heard at six by two witnesses. A nervous stranger had caught the evening train for Birmingham at Madeley Court station. He was carrying a bag, and was anxious to dry his newly-washed clothes. He seemed fearful of being followed, spoke with a foreign accent.

A hat had been left lying in the field where the murder was committed, the judge pointed out. Would an uncommonly tidy murderer, who had laid out the corpse as if for burial, have left the hat there, unless it was growing dark and he had missed it?

After a trial that became the longest in living memory, the jury were out for nearly two hours. They finally returned a verdict of not guilty. Harris was acquitted, to the relief of his friends.

The Old Man of Lower Prees Heath

In 1887 George Pickerill, a retired servant, was eighty years old. He lived alone in a two-roomed cottage in Lord Hill's timber-yard in Lower Prees. His daughter, Mrs Porter, who lived in Prees, came frequently to clean and cook for the old man. On November 12th. she turned up and couldn't get in. She was afraid that the old man had died—he had not been at all well on her last visit—so she called on James Adams, the works foreman, who lived close by, for help. The locked door defeated him, so he took out a pane from the bedroom window and climbed in.

He found the old man dead in a corner of the kitchen—but not of natural causes. His throat had been cut, and there were a dozen wounds to his face and head. A bloodstained butcher's knife belonging to the victim lay near the body.

When the police arrived they forced open the door with a poker. The key was afterwards found, apparently dropped by the murderer in his haste to get away. Near the house were found iron bars with blood and grey hairs on them. Pickerill's possessions had been rifled, but his money, hidden in secret drawers, was untouched.

The shocked people of the neighbourhood soon came to suspect a William Arrowsmith, a Mancunian, who was a distant relative of the old man and had been seen in the vicinity recently. His wife had gone to America, leaving him with three children, two of them deaf and dumb, whom he had parked with his sister, Mrs Myatt, in Denton.

Meanwhile, he had been working as a labourer in Newcastle, and living with a woman and her five children. Arrowsmith had recently visited old Pickerill at Prees and tried to leave two or three of these children with him.

Arrowsmith was spotted on the day of the murder walking away from Prees carrying three bundles of clothing bound up in differently coloured handkerchieves. In a few days evidence came in from pawnbrokers in Nantwich, Stockport, Hyde and Ashton-under-Lyme that a man had called wanting to pawn clothing. He had used different names, but it was almost certainly Arrowsmith each time.

It seemed he had also been asking his way to his sister's place in Manchester. Superintendent Edwards, of Whitchurch went there himself, and took lodgings with the sister under an assumed name. Soon afterwards, Arrowsmith walked in. Incriminating pawn tickets were found on him. He was even wearing some of the murdered man's garments.

He was charged with the murder of old Pickerill. At his trial he strongly protested his innocence, but was found guilty and sentenced to death. While awaiting execution he confessed his guilt to the prison chaplain and made a written confession, details of which could not, as a result of new rules, be divulged. He appeared penitent. At a late stage he was visited by his two sisters and Mrs Porter. He told them that he was grievously sorry for his great sin.

He was executed on a wet and snowy March day. These grisly affairs were no longer public spectacles, yet over five hundred people assembled outside the prison to see the black flag hoisted on top of the porter's lodge.

Tragic Feud at Whixall

In 1887, Elijah Bowers Forester and William Powell lived in Whixall. They were neighbours, but there was no love lost between them. In fact, their dislike of each other amounted to a feud, which erupted every now and again into acrimonious litigation. Forester charged Powell with stealing his dog. Powell accused Forester of stealing his chickens. Death brought the feud to a violent end.

The last act in the drama began with Powell taking down a gate belonging to Forester, which generated so much fury in the latter that he composed a song about his enemy. It went as follows:

> There was a man, an Indian red,
> Which all the neighbours do him dread,
> The cocks and hens begin to squeak
> When into the hen roost he does sneak.

Verses two and three were of similarly high literary quality. The fourth stanza ran:

> The wind blew well, the bushes were dry,
> Says he, my fortune I mean to try;
> To rob the insurance was his intent
> So he struck a match, and off it went;
> And when money he doth lack,
> Something has to go to rack;
> And to satisfy his foul desire,
> He set his own bedding on fire.

This might have remained a harmlesss release of bitterness had he kept it to himself. Instead, he took it into his head to march up and down outside his enemy's house, bawling out the words of this ditty at the top of his voice. Powell, growing rather weary of this boisterous performance, decided to go out and parley with him. His little daughter Rhoda was the last person to see him alive as he went out of the door into the dark.

Immediately afterwards there were two shots. Powell was found at once, with a large hole in his side. He died within minutes.

Domestic Tragedy at Baschurch

Charles Kynaston was a farmer at Fenemore Bank, Baschurch. He lived with his wife, five children, and the usual domestic and outdoor servants. But in 1887 all was not well in the home. For several years the marriage had been drifting on to the rocks. As a result of the disharmony, or perhaps as a prime cause of it, Betsy Kynaston had taken to drink.

Her husband had been advised to stop keeping beer in the cellar, but this would have been inconsistent with his position as head of a Victorian farming family. He therefore padlocked the cellar door and kept the key in his waistcoat pocket. But the thirsty lady took it when he was asleep. Finally, he maintained that it was impossible to hide it where she wouldn't find it.

The marriage had reached the stage where Charles and Betsy Kynaston were sleeping in separate rooms. The servants had witnessed violent quarrels, beatings, and a certain occasion when the farmer had put his wife out on a cold, dark winter's night with a child in her arms. Worse than that, perhaps, was the general belief that Charles was carrying on with a servant girl. His wife maintained that she had caught the pair in bed together more than once. On one occasion she had put a lighted lamp in the room as proof that she knew what was going on. Eventually Emma Brayne, the girl in question, was seen to be pregnant and was summarily discharged.

On the night of August 7th, according to the farmer, he was awakened by a loud bang. He jumped out of bed, shaken, and called to rouse the servant William Mathers, who was sleeping upstairs. The boy Brayne, Emma's brother, was also summoned. Kynaston, trembling with shock, asked them if they had heard a gun go off. He then led them directly to his wife's room where she was found to be dead, a gun lying beside her on the covers.

Dr Corke was called from Baschurch, and so were the police. The doctor made a careful study of Mrs Kynaston's injuries and the position of the gun. In his opinion the lady could not have committed suicide. The wound which had caused her death was in the wrong place.

The policeman agreed with him, and was confident that the ramrod lying on the bed could not have been used to pull the trigger. This, added to the local knowledge of the long-standing strife in the Kynaston household, led to the farmer's arrest.

Kynaston denied that he was the father of Emma Brayne's child. He had recently used the gun in the raspberry field, and afterwards left it in its accustomed place in the kitchen, with a charge in the barrel. Most people following the case were of the opinion that Kynaston had murdered his wife. However, there was insufficient evidence to convict the prisoner, and he was acquitted.

Double Killing at Clun

Charles Wells, a Clun butcher was concerned one afternoon in June, 1939, when his roundsman William Bufton was late in returning to base. Assuming Billy's little blue van must have broken down, Charles recruited his father and twelve-year-old son to accompany him, tossed a tow rope into his car, and drove off to look for the van.

Something seemed to urge him to try Churchbank. Sure enough, he came across the vehicle parked outside Rhos Cottage, Pen y Wern.

Mrs Jennie Venables, a regular customer, lived in the isolated grey stone cottage, some three miles from the little town. Her husband, a farm labourer, was known to cycle six miles daily to his work in Little Hagley.

Mr Wells got no response when he knocked on the cottage door, nor yet when he shouted. Peering in through the kitchen window, he was astounded to see the face of a woman on the floor under the table, and what looked like a pair of male feet. He pushed open the door and found Mrs Venables and his roundsman, still in his white smock, both apparently dead. Deeply shocked, he hurried away to inform the police.

As the good folk of Clun realized that something was up, another alarming report was circulating. George Owen, a county council roadman, who lived in a cottage with his invalid wife and daughter, and who was related by marriage to the murdered Bufton, had allegedly cut his own throat. He had been taken to Shrewsbury, an operation had been carried out on him, and he was expected to survive.

At the inquest, conducted at Bishops Castle by H. T. Weyman, senior coroner of England with 65 years' service, Wells the butcher described how he had found the bodies. Bufton had had half of his face blown away, and Mrs Venables a severe chest or abdominal wound. He had seen no gun.

Later, the roadman Owen, was charged with the murders. The next examination took place in the tiny Town Hall court in Clun. It was crowded for the ten-minute hearing, with a large number of people collected in the square. Owen smoked his pipe while he waited to be taken away.

At the magistrates' court in August, a witness reported hearing two shots at 2.15 p.m. on the day of the tragedy. It emerged that the cottage was on Owen's stretch of road and that he used to leave his tools there, and sometimes had meals there. Since no weapon was found at the scene, a third person had to be involved. The picture became clearer when a shotgun, both barrels fired, was found near Owen's house, and spent cartridges between the two dwellings. Owen had borrowed the gun for shooting rabbits.

Other witnesses testified to the roadman's dislike of Bufton. More than one had heard him threaten to kill the popular roundsman. He had apparently nursed a powerful objection to the time the younger man seemed to dally at the cottage. The doctor who had examined Owen's injury gave it as her opinion that it was self-inflicted.

At the Shropshire Assizes in November, before Mr Justice Lawrence, Owen was found unfit to plead. Appearing in court in a brown suit, with a muffler around his neck, he had taken scant interest in the proceedings. He was held to be suffering from feeble-mindedness and super-imposed dementia. He was ordered to be detained during His Majesty's pleasure, and was sent to a criminal asylum.

Horror at Wooferton

A tragedy at Wooferton which caused a widespread sensation in January, 1885, concerned a saw-sharpener called John Wright, who occupied with his wife a cottage on the old turnpike road. They had not got on well together for some time, and their relationship worsened when Eliza found herself another man. In her husband's words, when he confided in a neighbour:

'My wife has left me some two or three weeks, and she's gone to live with that old scamp of a Newman, a blacksmith at Aston. If she'd stop away and leave me, I wouldn't interfere with her in any way, but she comes here to do what she likes with me.'

When they quarrelled, which they frequently did, Eliza would go for her husband with a knife. She must have been fairly handy with it, for he appeared in public, this 50-year-old with a beetling forehead and a beard, with several scars on his face, the freshest treated with sticking plaster.

This presumably exhausted the husband's patience in the end, for one night he wrested the table knife from her grasp and cut her throat with it. He then lugged her to the bed and dumped her on it, getting blood all over his clothes in the process, washed his hands in a cheese box, and went to Police Sergeant Baynham to give himself up. That officer was away at a sale, so Wright came home, tied up his wife's jaw with a handkerchief, and laid himself down beside her to sleep.

In the morning he laid Eliza out, put a towel over her face and a woman's bodice over her feet, and set off again to give himself into custody.

He had shaken hands with customers at the refreshments rooms near Dinmore Station on the previous day, saying, 'I think this is the last night I shall have with you at Wooferton.' At the petty sessions he offered no defence. In a densely crowded court, he was committed for trial on a charge of wilful murder.

Appalling Murder at Wellington

In the early morning of February 1st, 1812, a boy found the body of a man in a stone quarry at Redlake, Wellington. The head had been cruelly battered and his throat cut. He was wearing clean, dry clothes, so he must have arrived in the steep-sided pit after the rain in the first part of the night had ceased. His name was William Bailey, a well-known local chap. Did he fall, or was he put? was the question.

Elizabeth Bowdler lived close to the new house of John Griffiths, cooper, about a quarter of a mile from the quarry. On the night before the discovery of the body she had been looking out of her window on to the road lit by Mr Botfield's ironworks. She saw Griffiths enter his new house and re-appear after a minute or so dragging 'a large parcel', which he left on the doorstep while he carried out a swift reconnaissance up and down the road. Seeming satisfied that the coast was clear, he fetched what looked like some clothing from the house, and threw it over his heavy bundle, which he dragged backwards around the corner of the new house, into which he had not yet moved.

John Bailey, a brother of the dead man, found keys in the pocket of the corpse, but no money and neither of his two watches. On entering his brother's house, he found clothing scattered about, and money apparently missing.

He had the body taken home from the quarry and got a warrant to search Griffiths's new house. There was a great deal of blood on the floor and stains on the walls and door-step. Sand had been sprinkled on the floor, an attempt had been made to scratch the stains from the walls, and a corner of the step had recently been chipped off. A passer-by had seen Griffiths approaching his house with both hands full of sand.

There was a vault, eight feet by four feet, beneath the floor. The only way to get into it was by taking up the floor slabs, which were nailed down. A lot of blood was found there which had apparently run down between the slabs. A handkerchief and shirt found among the coal turned out to belong to the deceased. But the most important discovery was the cooper's adze, which had blood on its point.

The surgeon, Mr W. Dunning, examined the body and found many injuries leading to serious loss of blood and fractures. He concluded that the victim had been struck violently many times with an adze.

When the news of the murder broke, Griffiths was at the home of William Rigby, who asked him several times if he would go with him to the scene.

'No,' said the cooper. 'I do not like dead bodies.'

The blood in the vault came from horseflesh, he said, for feeding the dog. The shirt he had bought in Birmingham—he couldn't understand how the initials W.B. had got on to it—and the handkerchief from a hawker. He had recently ground his adze, had happened to have money about him because trade had been good. Mary Dunning, for instance, had just paid him for work done with a 'Shifnal Bank £5 note'.

Elizabeth Bell deposed that she had seen the deceased sitting in the prisoner's house. Griffiths paid her a special visit the next morning to convince her that it had been somebody else. The local pawnbroker testified that Griffiths had pawned two watches, his wife's blankets and clothes. Nothing had been redeemed.

By now, the cooper must have begun to feel the pressure. He asked the surgeon if the deceased's wounds could have been caused by his falling into the pit. Not possible, was the unequivocal reply.

Only two citizens offered testimony in support of Griffiths. One had seen a quantity of horseflesh at the prisoner's new house. The other had sold him timber, for his trade and for his new house. He always paid regularly.

In a courtroom 'crowded to excess' for the trial, the jury took only a few minutes to return a verdict of 'guilty'. Calm up to this stage, Griffiths seemed 'greatly affected' when he heard his sentence, and burst into tears on reaching his cell. He confessed all on the following day.

On the scaffold he sang a hymn and exhorted the surrounding populace to 'take warning by his untimely fate'. He was then, in the journalist's euphemism, 'launched into eternity'.

The Case of the Wellington Taxidermist

Thomas Parton, aged 65, taxidermist, was living in 1885 with his wife and son Harry in Wrekin Road, Wellington. He was partial to whisky—sometimes two half-pints a day—and when in drink was given to whimsical actions, such as shouting 'murder!' at the top of his voice.

In June his wife, Emma, was in Worcester, and his son Harry in Llandudno. A kindly neighbour was looking after the old man. Both the travellers returned on the evening of the 12th. Emma turned up first, found the house empty, and had no key. She suspected that both of her men would be at their favourite pubs. She waited an hour and a half, then went to look for her husband. He wasn't at his usual watering-hole. But Harry was, and they went home together. Harry, was carrying his usual stick, a cane with a long, pointed horn handle at right angles to the shaft.

Later that night there were ructions in the Parton household. Neighbours heard sounds of violent quarrelling. From the back bedroom came old Mr Parton's not unfamiliar cry of 'murder!' Then after midnight mother and son emerged and told one of them that the taxidermist was dead. Mrs Parton explained.

'He has tumbled downstairs,' she said, 'and Harry has carried him upstairs.'

The sudden death of a well-known neighbour triggered speculation. Had the victim been sober? Had the shout of 'murder!' been anything more than the yell of a drunk?

Various people recalled seeing father and son quarrelling heatedly. Harry had been seen to knock his dad down in the garden 'among the beans'. The old man had sported black eyes coloured by Harry's fists.

Dr Calwell did a post-mortem on the body. He did not think the injuries were consistent with the deceased having fallen downstairs; he did not believe Harry could have carried the body back upstairs without help. Witnesses who had seen the deceased earlier on that same evening did not think he had been intoxicated. Calwell concluded that Mr Parton had died as a result of blows to the head from the handle of his son's cane.

Harry was committed on a charge of wilful murder, Emma as an accessory after the fact. At the outset the chief prosecutor said that he would produce no evidence against Emma, and she was discharged. Two senior surgeons appeared as witnesses for the defence. They disagreed with the Wellington surgeon. The injuries, they declared, could not have been made by the stick, but were consistent with falling downstairs. The man died from a general shock to the nervous system, they said. There was 'contusion of the brain, with greatly injured internal organs from continued intemperance.'

The jury very quickly brought in a verdict of not guilty. There was loud clapping in court, which angered the judge. 'Silence,' he commanded. 'Who dares to make that noise? This is not a theatre.'

Child Murder at Kynnersley

Joseph Bates, gasman at Apley Castle, was walking around Apley Castle Pool one morning in February, 1883, looking for duck eggs. His dog was attracted by a bundle lying in the shallow water some distance from the path. When Joseph retrieved it, he was horrified to find it contained the head of a girl aged about twelve.

He took it to the police station. Although news of the dreadful discovery spread like wildfire around the neighbourhood, it was three days before a cowman's wife named Isabella Hicks recognized the face as that of Mary Elizabeth Mayo, aged ten.

Sergeant Lloyd went to the Mayo home. The girl's father, Thomas, a groom-gardener, was out. Her mother stated that she had taken the child to Shrewsbury a fortnight previously, and then to stay with her grandmother at Yockleton. She would not, however, supply the address, and was arrested.

Thomas had by now been told of the gruesome find. He went back to work, where two policemen shortly came to see him. He told the same tale as his wife, was arrested and conveyed in a trap to Wellington police-station.

The gossip about the Mayos was that the parents had been habitually cruel to their children. They had both been married twice—Mrs Mayo to a John Williams, whom she had borne two sons before he died. Both boys had been adopted by the Yockleton granny. After Williams, Elizabeth had lived with a quack doctor, a well-known character in Wellington market. Tiring of him, she married Thomas, who was a widower with five children—Sarah Jane, William, Mary Elizabeth, Rosetta and Annie.

The Mayos had originally lived in New Street, Frankwell, Shrewsbury. There they had treated their children so badly that the neighbours had called in the police and Mrs Mayo was arrested. Both parents had been in custody for maltreating Mary Elizabeth, who was often bruised, filthy and emaciated. Thomas served twenty-one days in gaol. On his release he had been unable to find work, so he had moved with his brood to Kynnersley.

The cruel treatment of the children continued. Poor Mary Elizabeth ran away from home and sought protection with the family of a cowman. From what the child said it was obvious that her parents hated her. When her mother came to fetch her she said she was soon taking her to Shrewsbury Infirmary because she was poorly.

The prosecuting counsel in court suggested that on February 1st the deceased girl was beaten about the head until she died. She was then dismembered, some parts of her bundled up and put in the pool, other parts burnt. Mr and Mrs Mayo had been seen on the road to Shrewsbury, one carrying a basket, the other a bundle.

An hour later Mrs Mayo, now on her own, met the postman. The inventive lady told the letter carrier that she had been taking Mary Elizabeth to Shrewsbury and realized that she had left her purse on the table. She told the child to wait for her at the bottom of Apley Lawn while she went back to fetch it. Her husband noticed the purse, came to meet her with it, and then they had not been able to find the child.

This web of deceit was bound to find them out, but suspicion among the neighbours was allayed to some extent when Mary Elizabeth's brother William told them that his sister had been despatched all dressed up to the county town.

For quite some time the finding of the head was not linked with Mary Elizabeth's absence, although when the Mayo chimney caught fire a most unpleasant smell was noticed by many. The mother joined in the shocked discussion of the crime. She had the police station bill read to her, and afterwards for some reason seemed more calm in her mind.

The police continued an assiduous search for clues. They found another bundle in the same pool on the thirteenth. It contained the legs of a child. The chief constable personally searched the Mayo house. He found partially burnt bones in the ash hole under the grate and in the ash pit outside. There were spots of blood everywhere, and a coal hammer and a broomhook were confiscated.

Elizabeth Mayo decided that it was time to make a confession; her husband made his soon afterwards. Their stories were not consistent, so it was unclear who had been responsible for what.

As a result of one statement, the Severn was dragged from Chilton to Atcham Bridge. No fresh evidence was found.

The judge in his summing-up suggested that the mother was responsible, perhaps unintentionally, for the child's death, in which case she would be culpable of manslaughter. Her husband, an accessory after the fact, had mangled his own daughter's body in a vile and unspeakable manner.

The jury brought in a guilty verdict on both counts. Mrs Mayo got penal servitude for twenty years, Thomas prison with hard labour for eighteen months. The general feeling was that even if his cold-blooded brutality was a misguided attempt to protect his wife, he had got off lightly.

Treachery at Hopton Castle

During the Civil War, in 1644, Hopton Castle, belonging to a gentleman in the name of Wallop, was defended by a garrison of just over 30 men under the command of Colonel More of Linley Hall and Major Phillips. They were attacked by a substantially stronger force of Royalists commanded by Sir Lewis Kirke, of Ludlow. Despite stubborn resistance, the defenders began to find their situation untenable.

They had been battered by the artillery and they were running short of provisions. Their walls and their resolution were both being undermined.

Anxious to resolve the impasse and register a victory, the Royalist leader offered a bargain. If the garrison would surrender, he would spare their lives. At first this offer was contemptuously refused. When, as was inevitable, it had to be accepted, the King's officer failed to keep his word. To his undying shame, the desperately hungry soldiers, having laid down their arms, were stripped, tied back to back, and butchered in cold blood. Their bodies were thrown into a nearby pool.

The only reason for this action ever put forward arose from a rumour that the soldiers of the garrison had fired poisoned bullets.

The ruins of Hopton Castle are still to be seen, a rather grim sight nowadays. They stand as forlorn testimony to a signal act of treachery. Some say that the ghosts of the murdered soldiers are on occasion faintly visible wandering around the bleak walls at dusk.

What Really Happened in the Wood?

The case of Joseph Downing and Samuel Whitehouse, aroused intense interest in the vicinity of Hales Owen, Salop, in 1822. The two principals—Downing, a cow-leech (cow-doctor) and Whitehouse, a currier (dresser of tanned leather)—were friends of long standing. They lived about three miles apart, and each was married to the other's sister.

A mutual friend was Thomas Fox, blacksmith. Every year, the three of them were wont to meet at Fox's house and enjoy some shooting. Such a get-together was arranged for the third day of April. Whitehouse turned up first, at eight, riding his mare, bringing his gun and his spaniel with him. Downing did not arrive until ten. He, too, was on horseback. He intended to benefit from the blacksmith's arm by having the colt he was leading shod and the breech of the gun he was carrying enlarged.

The trio went off cock-shooting on that Wednesday morning, returning at mid-afternoon to put away two quarts of ale. The barrel was fixed, the colt shod, and the men went to look over a farm Whitehouse owned nearby. On their return they had something to eat, gossiped, and quaffed more ale.

At nine they were ready to set off home. Their way led through Beech Wood, where there was a carriage road, but an alternative route was available via a trig road, which was little more than a sheep track. As the two men approached the entry to the wood Downing realized he had left his adapted gun barrel in Fox's kitchen. He went back for it, calling to Whitehouse not to go without him, as the last time he had ridden through the wood after dark he had got lost. But Whitehouse did not wait.

Meanwhile Fox had retired to bed, only to be awakened at midnight to be told that a misfortune had befallen Whitehouse. At the Beech Tree public-house, only a hundred yards away, his recent guest was unconscious and mortally injured. Medical assistance had been called, so Fox rode to Downing's house on Whitehouse's mare. The two men came back through the wood together, examined the place where Whitehouse had been found, but could not see much. At the pub Whitehouse seemed to be hostile towards Downing, who nevertheless sent for his own surgeon to tend his apparently dying friend.

A young man called Aston now comes into the tale. He had stopped a riderless horse leaving the wood, ascertained that it belonged to Whitehouse, and ridden her back along the trig road until he came upon the man's body lying across the track, breathing hard, gun and spaniel beside him. He could not lift the unconscious Whitehouse, so rode on to Fox's for help.

Reinforced by Fox, Mrs Fox, their daughter and their servant, he returned to the scene. As they approached the spot, they heard a man 'hollow' and the sound of a horse galloping away.

When they reached Whitehouse, he was in a different position. He had either moved, or been moved. Now he lay on his back in a ditch, his clothing all awry. One breeches pocket was unbuttoned and empty; his watch and shot pouch were gone. Yet the stakes of a £2 wager, struck that afternoon, were untouched.

In court, where Downing was charged, one Ezekiel Dearns, a nailer, testified to having observed the comings and goings along the road outside his shop. There had been two strangers among the passers-by, and on his homeward journey Downing had been ahead of Whitehouse's galloping riderless mare.

There was strong testimony of the good feeling which had always existed between Downing and Whitehouse. Why would the former have wanted to harm his old friend?

Mr Justice Bayley pointed out that the trig road through the wood where Downing had already gone astray once was crossed and re-crossed by other tracks. It would have been easy for the horseman, distracted a little, perhaps, by the colt he was leading, to have taken a wrong turning and passed his friend unawares in the wood. The rider who was heard galloping away from the scene could not have been Downing, reported as having left the wood earlier.

The judge suggested that the dead man could have been fatally injured by an attacker using a crow-bar, or, had he been thrown by his horse, kicked by the frightened animal.

Downing was discharged. The court reporter noted that he left the Bar 'very much affected'.

Murder and Suicide at Ironbridge

One Saturday in November, 1887, there was an early morning commotion in Ironbridge and Madeley Wood when it became known that an elderly man had tried to murder his wife and then committed suicide.

The man was George Boucley, aged 60, whom the neighbours had observed acting strangely for some time. He and his wife had been in normal good health, their daughter Annie testified at the inquest. On the night before the tragedy they had been on quite good terms with each other.

Annie slept with her mother. On that dreadful night, she had been rudely awakened by her mother screaming. Annie leapt out of bed to see her father, in his night attire, standing over her mother with an axe in his hand. He struck his wife twice with it and then ran downstairs. Annie followed him, fearful of what he might be going to do next. He seized a razor and started upstairs again. When Annie attempted to hold him back, he threatened to use it on her.

Annie then ran into the street and shouted 'Murder!' Turning back towards the house she met her father thrusting her mother out through the door and throwing the axe at her. Annie helped her to a neighbour's house, where, streaming with blood, she was taken in by Sarah Lamb. Dr Proctor found her there, conscious but with four head wounds, one having penetrated the brain. Later she became unconscious and paralysed down the right side. Her face was so damaged as to be unrecognizable. She gasped out that she didn't know the reason for the brutal attack.

Meanwhile Boucley had returned to his bedroom and attempted to commit suicide. Police Sergeant Roberts found him, alive but sinking on his blood-soaked bed, the razor beside him. His throat had been cut three times, the windpipe severed.

No sooner was the inquest jury sworn at the Golden Ball than news was received that Boucley's wife had also died. The jury was re-sworn and the inquiry continued.

A neighbour, Thomas Wood, said he had heard Annie cry, 'You have killed my mother!' He had been disinclined to enter the house, Boucley being a dangerous fellow who had some time before given him a blow with a pick-axe, and three weeks earlier had stabbed his son.

Under questioning both Annie and the sheltering neighbour admitted that the deceased couple had been always quarrelling. Boucley had not threatened his wife on the night of the murder but 'he had often said he would put an end to her.'

The jury found 'wilful murder' against Boucley.

Blondie Jack of Shrewsbury

Folklore perpetuates the story of Jack Blondell, of Shrewsbury, who once lived within the castle precincts. He married six women in succession. Each of the first five, when he grew tired of her and wanted a change, disappeared from view and was never seen again. The sixth became concerned about what had happened to the fifth, who had been her sister.

She mentioned her suspicions to an alert watchman. This brisk fellow took her complaint seriously, and during his search of Blondell's hovel he came across a cupboard full of rotting human remains. He moved away, took a deep breath, and blew the whistle.

Bold Jack was taken into custody and a confession of his nefarious activities beaten out of him. He expiated his sins by swinging from a gibbet at Old Heath. Not many people know that his ghost, and possibly those of his hapless wives as well, haunts the castle to this very day.

Concealment of Birth at Petton

In March, 1902, Clara Beatrice Lowndes, aged 21, had worked for Mrs Susannah Cooke of Wackley Farm, Petton, for three years and she had been a good servant, but got pregnant.

Clara's mistress suspected her condition and challenged her, but was told that there was nothing amiss. While the girl was away enjoying a fortnight's holiday at Christmas, 1901, Mrs Cooke wrote to her and asked her not to return if she were with child. Clara did return and, when taxed again, denied she was pregnant and refused to see a doctor.

On March 24th Clara rose as usual at five, did some milking and suckled some calves. While preparing breakfast she complained of a pain and her employer gave her some pills and told her to have a day in bed. A little later Mrs Cooke saw Clara in an outhouse and noticed some blood on her clothing. Had she had a child? No, replied Clara, the pills 'made the blood come to my mouth'. She asked for water to wash out her mouth. Mrs Cooke's niece, Mary Elizabeth, went to keep an eye on her, and the ailing girl was finally sent to bed.

Mrs Cooke went out again and examined the outhouse, where she saw what seemed to be the feet and legs of a baby. She went upstairs at once and accused Clara of having given birth.

'Oh, missus,' sobbed the girl, 'don't say nothing. No one will know if you don't tell them.'

Police Constables Rudge and Bolderston were called to Wackley and found the dead body of a female child in the outhouse.

Dr Bathurst was summoned from Ellesmere. The doctor found the baby's mouth and throat tightly stuffed with paper. The thin edge of the wedge of paper was fixed into the oesophagus, and needed a steady pull to remove it. It could not possibly have been pushed in by the child itself. At the post mortem it was confirmed that death was caused by asphyxia due to paper in the throat.

Clara was committed for trial at Shropshire Assizes. Mrs Cooke testified that she had found her hard-working and respectable. She would willingly take her on again if she had the chance.

Defending counsel argued that the child might not have had a separate existence and that Clara was not in a fit mental state at the time to realize what she was doing. The judge was sympathetic. Considering all the evidence, he said, the jury might find the appropriate charge was concealment of birth. Clara was found guilty on that count and was sentenced to six months' imprisonment in the second division.

Dunned to Death

The poisoning of William Mabbot, aged 37, a married man with three children, by William Samuels, 24, in 1886 qualifies as a Shropshire murder because both men belonged to Shrewsbury, but the actual murder took place in Welshpool. The motive for the crime, on the face of it, was rather flimsy—an outstanding debt of 16 shillings.

Mabbot had been employed by grocers Debac and Sheaff, of Shrewsbury. He lived in Barker Street, and his job was to travel to towns in Shropshire and Montgomeryshire on fair days and sell his firm's goods. On June 14th he went to his employer's shop in Welshpool where Samuels had a business dealing in provisions.

Samuels had worked for Debac and Sheaff five years earlier, for just over twelve months. When he then started in business on his own account, he bought stock from that firm, incurring a debt of nearly £8. Mabbot had been told to get that money as soon as he could and to extend to Samuels no more credit. This turned out to be no easy assignment, but by the time of the murder the sum outstanding had been reduced to 16 shillings. It is a trifle difficult to understand why this should have provided the motive for such an extreme step.

At the trial at the Montgomeryshire Assizes at Newtown it emerged that Samuels had on several occasions before the murder attempted to buy strychnine under assumed names, succeeding a week before the murder. On the day of the murder, Mabbot asked Samuels when he was going to clear off the balance of the debt. Samuels made an excuse to leave the room. When he re-appeared he was bringing his visitor a pint of porter.

The unsuspecting Mabbot took a good draught, became ill, and died within half an hour. It couldn't be termed a well thought out murder attempt, for there were traces of strychnine left in the bottom of the jug.

Samuels was found guilty. The death sentence was pronounced by Mr Justice Groves. His execution was the first to take place in Shrewsbury for 18 years.

Cold-Blooded Murder in Oswestry

John Davies (70) and his wife had been married for thirty-six years. Their life together had not been very happy, largely (according to the neighbours) because of Davies's violent behaviour after drinking bouts.

He was a poultry dealer living in Llanrhaiadr and trading in Oswestry market. Eventually the couple moved to live in Oswestry. Here the domestic disharmony seems to have worsened. The neighbours reported often hearing Mrs Davies screaming. In the end she applied for a separation order. At the hearing Mr Davies told the magistrates how her husband used to hit her in the stomach and threaten to kill her.

One day, when their relationship was at a low ebb, a passing policeman noticed that Davies had put all the furniture out into the street. He made him put it all back. Among the bits and pieces the police officer noticed a razor. Concerned by the 'demoniac look' on Davies's face, he put it in 'a place of safety' and forgot about it until the name Davies came sensationally into the news.

After the breakup, Davies was accommodated in Oswestry Workhouse for some time. There had been a complaint that while he was being maintained by the rates he was buying and selling fowls in Oswestry market. On October 6th, 1902, he was discharged from the workhouse.

Despite his age, Davies was at that time tall, fit and quite strong. It seemed that a recent family crisis had arisen from the death by drowning in Malta of a soldier son. A considerable sum of money became due to the parents but they had been unable to agree on how to divide it.

On that day, Davies was seen in Llys Lane. His wife left her house, caught sight of him, and set off in the opposite direction. He said to Mr Hughes, who was passing:

'I don't know what's the matter with that bloody woman. She won't talk to me, but I will make her talk just now.'

He made haste to catch her up.

Coming in the opposite direction were Thomas Bromley, of Babbinswood, and his brother-in-law, Thomas Owen. They were returning from Oswestry market, along the footpath via Coney Green to Llys Lane. After they had passed the railway they heard screams and then they met Davies and his wife.

'What's up?' asked Owen.

'We are husband and wife,' replied Davies, walking on, as if that explained everything.

After moving on another twenty yards there were renewed screams, and the two out-of-towners turned back, alarmed. They were horrified to see Davies take a knife from his pocket and plunge it into his wife's chest. He had his left arm about the woman and struck with his right. Bromley and Owen ran to the spot but were not in time to prevent the fatal blow. Owen helped up Mrs Davies, who staggered a few yards and then fell.

Davies now attempted to take his own life. He said at his trial that his knife had proved not sharp enough. Owen knocked him down, and there followed a terrible struggle between the two men. At that point a railwayman, Robert Jones, came along and helped Owen to hold the murderer down. The knife was taken from him.

When Davies quietened down he said he hadn't done it—she had scratched herself on a briar. Leave me alone, he said repeatedly. I want to die, please kill me.

In addition to the fatal chest wound penetrating the heart, the poor woman's face had been slashed by the knife and the flesh 'hung down like a curtain'. The men from Babbinswood—'brave citizens' the newspaper reporter called them—stayed to hold the murderer until Superintendent Lewis, P.C. Diggory and P.C. Palmer arrived and took Davies into custody.

When charged by the Superintendent, Davies said, 'I am sorry.' Mrs Davies's body was taken to the cottage hospital, where she was pronounced dead, and removed to the borough mortuary.

At the trial the prosecution alleged that the crime had been premeditated, the knife re-ground. Davies had had no money on him at the time of the murder. Presumably the motive for the attack had been his wife's refusal to give him any, after the workhouse guardians had stopped him from trading in the market.

When the prisoner was removed to Shrewsbury Gaol by the 7 p.m. train, the morbid interest of the general public was demonstrated by throngs of people on the station approaches and platform.

At the Shropshire Assizes Davies appeared as a rather feeble, white-haired old man who pleaded guilty in a low voice. The doctors agreed that he had not been responsible for his actions when he committed the murder. Always singular in manner, he had become unable to concentrate and suffered from insomnia. His condition was degenerating. He was found guilty, but insane.

Poaching at Cleobury Mortimer

In the year 1832 Sir Edward Blount, Bart., owned an extensive estate at Bayton, in the parish of Cleobury Mortiner. The head gamekeeper was John Bannock, who on the night of November the 27th was sitting in the Cross Keys public-house enjoying his pint. Among the other habitués were the brothers William and John Handley and an accomplice bearing the undistinguished name of Jones. These three, seeing Bannock settled in the pub, decided that it was a good opportunity to go after a pheasant. But Bannock was suspicious, and as soon as the poachers had left he went to 'collect a force' in order to 'watch the cover'. While the three miscreants were assembling two guns and the materials required to fire them, the gamekeeper and his three underlings repaired to a cover known as 'Peggy's Hole'. Here they drew a blank, and set off for home, disappointed.

Just after midnight they heard a shot in a second cover, called from its shape the 'Shoulder of Mutton'. They hurried away in that direction. The poachers had been in the coppice first, and William Handley had shot a hen pheasant, which Jones pocketed. Now the two groups were converging. Bannock heard the sound of sticks cracking and halted. Then a man cried 'Ba!', and was answered by another with the same call. The gamekeeper saw the second man raise his gun. He was felled then by a charge which impelled thirty-three shots into his face, three through his right eye, blinding it. He cried, in agony:

'Lord, have mercy upon me: I am shot!'

A mocking voice chanted 'O Lord!' three times.

Upon this the three poachers fled. Jones, very much the follower during the entire episode, gave much detailed evidence at the subsequent inquest. He had carried the tools—the ramrod, the stick and the hammer. The Handleys had each carried a gun, but John's had misfired. Jones was sure that it was William who had fired at the gamekeeper because the flash had lit up his clothing. Leaving the scene of the incident, Jones had flung away the equipment he had been carrying. Cross-examined, he reported William's statement to the effect that he would shoot rather than be taken.

Seven other witnesses corroborated Jones's evidence. The jury found William Handley guilty of attempted murder, his brother not guilty. In his summing-up the judge told William that his was 'a most heinous offence . . . attempting to destroy the life of a fellow creature. It makes me sick,' he went on, 'to tell a young man like you, in the bloom of health and in the figure of youth, that . . . your life must atone for the offence you have committed.'

William Handley was executed over the lodge in front of the County Gaol on the 6th of April, 1833.

The unctuous writer in the *Salopian Journal* of the day wrote:

'His fate should be a warning to those numerous desperadoes who have for some time infested this and other counties, and so often added to the crowded state of our prisons, and who, pursuing the profitless and dangerous practice of poaching, are led on, step by step, to the commission of other crimes, and until, as in the present instance, their lives become . . . forfeited to the offended laws of their country.'

Double Tragedy on the Stiperstones

Early in the morning of Good Friday, 1940, two unmarried brothers, both barytes miners, were found dead in a sunken road leading to a disused mine at The Bog, near Minsterley. Thomas Perkins was aged 30, Edward 12 years younger. They both had gunshot wounds in the head.

It appeared from the evidence that Edward had shot his brother between the eyes from a distance of two or three feet. Thomas could not, decided the local experts, have pulled the trigger himself. Edward's wound was blackened and scorched, suggesting that the muzzle of the weapon had actually been touching his head when it was fired. The gun, still in Edward's grasp, was 'broken'. It seemed that the younger man, who was quite long in the arm, had bent over the gun and pulled the trigger. As the weapon was very old, it 'broke' with the recoil and fell beside Edward as he collapsed.

The tragedy had been discovered by Mrs Emma Betton, from the Bog Gate. Passing the men's home at The Hostel, she saw the door open and the curtains drawn. At the sunken road she saw the bodies, shouted, and got no reply. Back at their house, another shout brought no response, so she hurried to tell Derwas Johnson, the licensee of the Miner's Arms, with considerable agitation, of what she had seen. He called the police.

The shocked villagers of that mining community found it difficult to establish a convincing cause of the tragedy. The two brothers were generally on the best of terms. They had lived contentedly at The Hostel, with a woman coming in to clean for them and their laundry 'sent out'. A friend's wife, Mrs Richards, prepared their food for them. They were sons of the late Mr and Mrs Perkins of The Squilver, near Wentnor. Their brother Jack, who was living in Devon, testified that they were used to handling a gun.

The only reason that the locals could come up with for the mystifying tragedy was that Edward had for some time been plagued with severe toothache, and this had made him depressed. His face had been badly swollen, and he had had to wait for the infection to subside before he could have the offending teeth removed.

A cousin had had a drink with the brothers only days before the tragedy, when they both seemed normal, reasonably sober, and were 'off after birds', a term implying night-time poaching. But on the night before Good Friday, Ted had expressed himself to be 'ramping mad' with pain. George Betton found him complaining about his neck and jaw. 'He didn't seem to have any life in him,' he said.

At the enquiry, held at the Town Hall, Bishops Castle, the jury decided that Edward had murdered his elder brother and then committed suicide.

The Westbury Murder

Richard Wigley, a 54-year-old Shrewsbury butcher at the turn of the last century, was a large man. He was born into his business, and for some time prospered. But his married life was unhappy. He began to drink heavily, his business collapsed, and he and his wife went their separate ways. A maintenance order was made against him, but he was irregular in his payments.

Eliza Mary Bowen, at 23 less than half of Wigley's age, was born at Llanfair, Montgomeryshire, and came to work at the Lion Inn, Westbury, where they got to know each other in 1899. In the following year she moved to Cound, to work as housekeeper for a farmer. At that time Wigley was employed as a butcher at Cross Houses. Bowen and Wigley 'kept company'; he used to take her out on two or three nights a week. He told his employer, who commented on Eliza being so friendly with a married man, that he 'was very fond of the woman'.

When Miss Bowen left Cound, Wigley found digs for her in Shrewsbury. Here he visited her regularly during her six-week stay. In August, 1901, she went back to Westbury to work for William Vaughan, the farmer who owned the Lion.

But for some reason she no longer welcomed Wigley's visits. After two visits, and she wrote to ask him not to come again. 'Dear Dick,' the letter ran, 'I hope to see you soon at Shrewsbury.' She sent her love, and added a P.S: 'Be sure you don't came here again.' Wigley kept the letter, as we shall see.

Eliza went to Shrewsbury only twice in the following three months. Wigley, always a passionate fellow, interpreted this coolness to mean the existence of a rival. Increased drinking fuelled his jealousy. Eliza, he told his landlady, was the only friend he had in the world and, as he later told the Westbury policeman, he was determined that 'no one else shall have her'.

On Saturday, November 3rd, he left his Hill's Lane lodgings very early and walked the nine miles to Westbury, taking alcoholic refreshment as available on the way. This cost him 2s 4d, out of the 2s 6d he had obtained from the sale of his tools. At the Lion he had several more drinks.

At this time only Eliza Bowen and one other servant, Ellen Richards, were in the house. Wigley caught Eliza in the passage and put his arm around her. The girl resisted this advance and told Ellen to fetch the village policeman. Wigley released her. Eliza went back to the bar, then left it to fetch something from the cellar. Wigley followed her, grabbed her by the arm, and held her firmly against the wall. Ellen, come to see what was causing the commotion this time, was horrified to see Wigley draw a clasp knife from his pocket with his free hand and flourish it in his victim's face. Ellen ran out, screaming for help.

In a few moments Eliza was tottering towards the door, bleeding profusely from a dreadful throat wound. She scrabbled at the wall for support, and fell senseless, and expired.

Ellen's screams brought Bob Rogers, the village blacksmith, with one or two others, running up to the inn to see what was afoot. Wigley came out to meet them.

'I have done it, lads,' he said. 'I have done it for love. I had come on purpose to do it, and am ready to swing.'

This statement he denied at his trial. But he had repeated it on the day of the murder to the village policeman and to Superintendent Elcock. Furthermore, he had scrawled a confession on the back of the envelope which had contained Eliza's letter, and left it in the bar. He seemed cool and collected immediately after the dreadful deed, and allowed himself to be held by the blacksmith until the local constable arrived to arrest him.

A Mr Bosanquet was instructed by the judge to defend Wigley, but only at the last moment. With little time for preparation, counsel entered a plea of insanity. It seemed that Wigley's mother had been in an asylum more than once. But the case against him was too strong, and included the fact that Wigley had told several people that he intended to murder Eliza Bowen. His hanging on the 18th of March, 1902, was the first execution at Shrewsbury jail for fourteen years. The barmaid's bloodstained handprint on the wall was impossible to remove. Only when the pub was demolished and a modern replacement built did the imprint finally disappear. So they say.

The Atcham Murder

Towards the end of 1953 Desmond Donald Hooper, a 27-year-old gardener, was tried for the murder of twelve-year-old Betty Selina Smith. Both accused and victim had been living, at the time of Betty's death four months earlier, in a camp at Atcham, three and a half miles from Shrewsbury.

Hooper, a married pigeon-fancier with children, worked at Copthorne Barracks. Betty had been to his home a few times. Hooper liked her because she was good with his children. In court he said that she was not as modest as she might have been. She enjoyed socials, as they were called, at her school and in the camp where she lived.

On the night of the murder Betty went to the Hooper home to collect some magazines. Mrs Hooper was out. What happened later was a matter of disagreement between the numerous witnesses called to testify in court.

Hooper claimed that he sent Betty home. Then, leaving a note for his wife to tell her that he had gone to look for pigeons, he walked to Attingham Home Farm, where he spent an hour and a half doing just that. He failed to retrieve any, because (he said) they were high in the rafters and he hadn't a ladder.

By this time Betty's mother, Mrs Webb, had turned up at the Hoopers on her bicycle. Betty had not come home. While she and Mrs Hooper debated their next move, Hooper arrived, seemingly distraught. He expressed surprise and disquiet at Betty's disappearance. The three of them went off to look for her, Mrs Webb resolving to inform the police if the girl were not found before eight o'clock in the morning.

The prosecution maintained that Hooper and Betty had gone out together, the girl wearing a blue pinstripe jacket belonging to Hooper, and had walked a couple of miles to an air shaft above a tunnel connected with the Shropshire Union Canal. Here, for some reason never made clear, Hooper had strangled Betty with his tie, and when she was close to death had dropped her head first down the air shaft into the water below.

Her body was found two days later. Near the top of the air shaft lay a blue pinstripe jacket, possibly overlooked in panic in the dark.

There was much vagueness, loss of memory and contradiction between the various witnesses. Hooper disclaimed the ownership of the abandoned jacket and of the lethal tie. Neither Mr Harris, the farmer with the pigeons, nor Mrs Lewis, whose bedroom overlooked the stockyard, had been aware of Hooper looking for pigeons and the normally wakeful dogs had not barked. A motorist remembered passing a couple on the road near the air shaft late at night—a man and a girl wearing an ill-fitting jacket.

An unusual feature of the trial was the hearing of evidence from Hooper's seven-year-old son—not sworn testimony, of course—that he had plainly heard Betty being sent home by his father. Unfortunately for Hooper, the boy later admitted that he had been coached in what he had to say.

Hooper was found guilty of murder. There was an appeal, which was disallowed, and he was hanged at Shrewsbury on 20th January, 1954.

George Riley

George Riley, a 21-year-old assistant butcher, was living in the Copthorne district of Shrewsbury in the autumn of 1960. On a certain Friday night in October he came home from work, having, according to his father, bought savings stamps on the way, and gave money to his mother as his contribution to the housekeeping expenses.

After tea, he went out with his friend Tony Brown in Brown's car. Together they visited four public-houses. There was some discrepancy later in the accounts of the amount of drink consumed, but Riley claimed to have put away eight to nine pints of beer and eight whiskies and orange. It was said during his trial at Stafford that it was far more than he had ever drunk before. He may have hoped that this would to some extent explain what happened later.

When the pubs shut, Riley and Brown moved on to a dance at the Sentinel Works at Harlescott. There Riley fell out with a Laurence Griffiths, and they were reported wrestling on the floor. Afterwards Riley was involved in two or three not very serious fights. He was apparently in a lively mood. Other people at the dance, including two policemen, judged that Riley had had plenty to drink but was not drunk.

The two young men eventually set off home, dropping a friend on the way, and arrived at Riley's place at about 1.30 a.m. At each stop Riley got out of the car and was able to stand without difficulty.

When his friend had driven off, according to Riley, he discovered that he had left his house key in his other suit. The house doors being locked, he made his way to the garage and fell asleep on a settee that was stored there. He wrote in his original statement that he woke up in the early morning, saw the dining-room light on, knocked on the window and was admitted by his brother Terry. He went up to bed and fell asleep again. In the morning, his shoes and trousers were seen to be muddy and grass-stained.

In a house across the road lived Mrs Smith, a slightly-built, middle-aged widow known to Riley. On the evening of the Sentinel dance her sister, Miss Olive Martin, who lived nearby, had visited her, leaving before half-past seven.

The next morning Miss Martin telephoned her sister, but could get no reply. She called at the house at about 10 a.m., but could get no answer. She knocked up a neighbour. Then, accompanied by a Sergeant Bean, she went round to the back of the house. A pane of glass had been broken in the French window. Sergeant Bean used the opening to insert his hand and lift the latch. He let Miss Martin in through the front. She went upstairs; there was a piercing scream. She had seen 'a grim and grisly sight'. Her sister was on the bedroom floor, apparently dead, savagely battered about the face, her head in a pool of blood. Her nightdress was almost torn off her body. Some of her teeth had been knocked out. George Riley was charged with murder.

At the trial, the defence claimed that Riley's first statement was inadmissible evidence. He had not been warned nor told that he didn't have to answer questions. He had not signed the statement. The accused wrote out a second statement, in which he told a different story which amounted to a confession. Indeed, he is alleged to have said at the time: 'I am signing my death warrant, aren't I?'

He had entered Mrs Smith's house in his befuddled state, he recollected, having spent more money than he intended. He had been to the house for change in happier days, and knew that the widow kept her cash in a handbag upstairs. Ironically, on this occasion there was a mere three shillings and sevenpence halfpenny in the purse in the bedroom.

Mrs Smith had jumped up in bed when Riley entered, shouted, and clung on to him. He had struck her violently in the face. When she fell, he had delivered more blows, kneeling. A ring he wore had done the worst of the damage.

Riley claimed that Mrs Smith had not been dead when he left her, that all he had wanted was money—there had been no question of a sexual motive—and that he was so drunk that he was not in full control of his actions. He had become frightened, left the house and made off across the fields behind the house until he found himself near The Grapes Inn at Bicton. This explained why on his return home his shoes had been muddy and his trousers wet and grass-stained.

The jury found Riley guilty of murder, and he was sentenced to be hanged. An appeal was disallowed, but right up to the last moment there was hope of a reprieve. Riley was the last man to be hanged in Shrewsbury. Many remember the racket that went on at the prison on the night before the execution by inmates who felt sympathy for the condemned young man and dismay at the sentence. They expressed their feelings in any way they could, by lighting small fires and banging metal.

The Shrewsbury Rose-Grower

On the 21st of March, 1984, Miss Hilda Murrell, an elderly, much-respected rose-grower, was abducted from her home in Sutton Road, Shrewsbury, where she lived alone. Her dead body, which had been savagely mutilated with a knife, was found three days later in a small wood near a beauty spot overlooking the town. She had apparently died of hypothermia where she lay, a quarter of a mile across a cornfield from a quiet lane. Her Renault car, which her assailant had used to transport her to a spot near where she was found, lay abandoned in a ditch.

The sensational news of the ghastly death of this remarkable old lady came as a severe shock to local people, even to those who up to that point had been unaware of her existence. Police enquiries established that Miss Murrell had been out shopping with her car. She had called back at her home to change before going out to lunch. An intruder, who might have been aware of her lunch appointment but had not expected her to return home first, was either already in the house or followed Miss Murrell in. Either way, the place was systematically searched and money taken. It appears that her captor then drove the old lady in her own car out of town and on to Haughmond Hill. Whether she fought with him and aroused his anger is still a matter for speculation. When, or how, she was carried, or dragged, 500 yards across a field, and whether one or more persons were involved, also remains conjectural.

Several theories to explain the motive for the murder have been put forward—chief among them the idea that Miss Murrell's opposition to the building of a second nuclear reactor at Sizewell had caused concern at a very high level.

It was also speculated that Miss Murrell's nephew, Lt. Commander Green, had inside knowledge of matters concerning the sinking of the Argentinian cruiser Belgrano during the Falklands War. Had there been copies of vital documents in her possession?

There were, however, sexual overtones to the affair, difficult to put into context unless the attacker were a common-or-garden psychotic.

Perhaps one day the truth underlying the murder of Miss Murrell will emerge. Meanwhile, the crime remains unsolved, and speculation has more or less ground to a halt. This may simply be due to the passage of time; or maybe because certain people with a secret to keep have done so rather well, the crime remains unsolved.